T0149591

OUR INNER CHILD CONNECTION

OUR INNER CHILD CONNECTION

Live Your Dreams Trusting Your Own Inner Wisdom

SANDY KENNEDY

BALBOA.
PRESS

A DIVISION OF HAY HOUSE

Balboa Press books may be ordered through booksellers or by contacting:

Balboa Press
A Division of Hay House
1663 Liberty Drive
Bloomington, IN 47403
www.balboapress.com
1 (877) 407-4847

Because of the dynamic nature of the Internet, any web addresses or
links contained in this book may have changed since publication and
may no longer be valid. The views expressed in this work are solely those
of the author and do not necessarily reflect the views of the publisher,
and the publisher hereby disclaims any responsibility for them.

The author of this book does not dispense medical advice or prescribe the use
of any technique as a form of treatment for physical, emotional, or medical
problems without the advice of a physician, either directly or indirectly. The
intent of the author is only to offer information of a general nature to help
you in your quest for emotional and spiritual well-being. In the event you use
any of the information in this book for yourself, which is your constitutional
right, the author and the publisher assume no responsibility for your actions.

Any people depicted in stock imagery provided by Thinkstock are models,
and such images are being used for illustrative purposes only.
Certain stock imagery © Thinkstock.

Interior illustrations: Tom Quinn
www.quinntheartist.com

Print information available on the last page.

ISBN: 978-1-5043-9211-2 (sc)
ISBN: 978-1-5043-9210-5 (hc)
ISBN: 978-1-5043-9212-9 (e)

Library of Congress Control Number: 2017918030

Balboa Press rev. date: 02/21/2018

DEDICATION

This book is dedicated to everyone who seeks
a better quality of life,
greater harmony in your relationships,
more moments of peace and joy, more
playtime and relaxation;
a life that fulfills your dreams and desires, and
a life that is lived free from strife and worry.
May you find answers that fulfill and uplift you,
by trusting the wisdom of your own heart-felt
thoughts and feelings.

CONTENTS

INTRODUCTION

Our Inner Child Connection is the culmination of a long fifty plus years of self-interest studies in the observation of daily life, world history, science, nature, and religions of the world; along with a dental assisting career; followed by an even longer government agency, public-sector real estate career; then a bachelor's degree in applied behavioral analysis psychology and a master's degree in rehabilitation counseling. Here's what I have learned through the years: All of the knowledge gained through external experiences pales in the light of what we already know internally about living a good life, when we allow ourselves to be guided by our feelings and our quiet inner voice of wisdom.

A person's age or formal education matters not when connecting with our feelings and our inner-wisdom. The feelings of pain, butterflies, and nausea in our gut and stomach in reaction to external forces are messages from our inner wisdom. The same is true for the feelings of happiness, joy, peace, kindness, and creativity coming from our heart-center where LOVE and our Inner-Child aspects are seated.

When we combine our external knowledge with our internal feelings and wisdom, life experiences take us to amazing places of peaceful living and joyful happiness. There is an easy way to tryout these concepts. They are presented in *Our Inner Child Connection* as tools and exercises designed to take our inner-journey one step at a time. Practice one tool or exercise until it becomes a natural way of being. Then try another one that brings you feelings of happiness, safety, peace, or some other uplifting value. One step equals one change.

Here are some thoughts to consider: What if the love in our hearts, the feeling of love we were born with had not been altered or corrupted by the outer world? What if that pure innocent love was protected and nurtured throughout our lives? What if our thoughts were honored and respected without critical judgment, and we could safely feel the freedom to express our true feelings? What if we could go through life without putting on layer after layer of the protective shell we use to guard our most vulnerable inner-self? We can have all of these good things restored to our lives.

Within each of us is a resource, an inner guide. Our heart-centered inner guide access opens by reflecting on and then describing our feelings. Feelings of being safe and protected start with our thoughts, with our intention to be safe and protected. Thoughts and intentions are followed by making action decisions, by feeling our feelings and following the guidance from our heart-centered inner wisdom. With practice, we gain the feeling of having a greater sense of safety. This supports our self-confidence so that we can be more genuinely open and authentic in our interactions. Our feelings are the Inner-Child place inside each of us that holds the loving emotions and joy we experienced as young children. This is the residence of our Inner-Child, who is innocently and openly honest, kind, caring, compassionate, and always without judgment.

What if we really could return to those early days of being in love with life? What if we could actually be true to ourselves, enjoy ourselves and enjoy life, all in a way by safely shedding our protective shell, as we navigate through daily life? Hold those thoughts while enjoying the offerings in this book. It is filled with reminders, tools, and activities designed to recapture our trust in life, to fulfill our dreams, and to develop the courage for opening our hearts to greater love and joy in our daily lives.

The tools offered in *Our Inner Child Connection* prompt a wholly personal investigation between our inner self and our social self. They present a query for discovering how to bring these two aspects of ourselves into closer alignment. The goal is to enjoy greater peace of mind and a sense of calm and happiness that come from feeling safe and protected –and loved.

Two key elements are:

- Living the wonderful, highest vision daily life of dreams-come-true is free of charge. This dream life is first created from within our thoughts and then expressed through our actions.
- Anyone can achieve their highest ideal for living a life of happiness, regardless of any current beliefs in barriers. Everything we put our minds toward accomplishing is possible to achieve. Barriers are just thoughts, ideas that we cling to. And thoughts can be changed, just by choosing to change them.

For example: breaking the barrier of an unwanted habit is a personal decision. What was daily life like before the habit began? Make the decision to stop the habit and return to the rhythm of life prior to starting the habit. The success of breaking a habit depends upon the quality of life a person desires.

We all have the ability within us for dissolving barriers and to feel our inner Joy and Peace. Visible results for breaking an unwanted habit or some other life-restricting barrier begins with our thoughts and our free-will decisions. Our outer world fulfillment of desires unfolds like flower petals –sometimes going unnoticed until on display as a fully opened flower. The beauty of the flower is a personal decision. How high have you set your quality of life vision?

It helps to stay focused in the present moment, to enhance awareness of the ever-unfolding changes in daily life. Staying focused in the present moment takes much practice. For that reason, important messages presented in *Our Inner Child Connection* are often repeated. This is to reinforce the necessity of keeping the messages in our thoughts as often as possible.

Gratitude and appreciation are examples. As we practice being grateful for and appreciating events and activities throughout each day, we tend to find even more things to be grateful for and to appreciate. With continued practice, this exercise could eventually become all-encompassing throughout each day. In a very good way, this is a life-changing exercise for our self-perception and our perception of the world we live in. When we are grateful and appreciative, life boomerangs back to us gratitude and appreciation in surprising ways that forever improve our views of life.

The key principle: Happiness comes from within our being. We choose to be happy. Our kind and loving thoughts bring happiness into our lives. The best days we can experience are as simple as the quality of our thoughts. Our lives are governed by our thoughts. Let's practice elevating our thoughts to our highest vision of life enjoyment.

Effort was made to assemble this book into short information segments that could be introduced, mulled over and digested. Each chapter serves as a simple form of the collective whole, of the overarching message of *Our Inner-Child Connection* that every person is an important thread in the fabric-of-life on Earth. Our Inner-Child exploration focuses on tuning-in more closely with our feelings and physical reactions, as we respond to external interactions and information.

The chapters are oriented toward all of us living the most peaceful and joyously happy life possible. Global change happens one person at a time. Each of us has a role, a purpose in life that is based on our individual interests and talents. In some way, everyone is important to the whole of life on Earth. *Our Inner Child Connection* urges the reader to seek happiness each day and to live without judgment. We are each such unique individuals, that we never know the full history behind another's behavior, including those who are closest to us.

It is best for everyone to withhold judgment, starting with ourselves. Our feelings are uplifted when we support our daily actions and forgive our personal errors. These are acts of kindness that promote a life of peace and happiness. All of the messages in *Our Inner Child Connection* funnel together into a basic message of being kind and considerate to ourselves and to others, of giving up control and allowing life to flow freely, without inserting dams and diversions along the way.

Daily life in this age of well-developed electronic communication is a continuous stream of information without identifiable beginnings or endings. It has been said that the more we know, the more we realize that there is always more to know. It's no wonder we get bogged down trying to make sense of it all. Our lives are mired in a tiresome blur of constantly trying to intellectualize endless input being blasted onto our senses.

All the while, our Inner-Child is just interested living in the present moment joy of life. Our Inner-Child lives with reckless abandon, immersed in the *love of love*. Our Inner-Child is that place found in our heart-center where we feel happiness, even joy. It is where our feelings of *love* are centered. It is where we find peace and a safe haven. By trusting our heart-centered feelings, we learn to be fearless, and to be our most authentic selves in our daily interactions.

Why spend so much of our precious lifetime being drawn into making daily life complicated and painful, when our Inner-Child has great wisdom to guide our thoughts and actions? Please enjoy the journey found within.

-Sandy Kennedy

Be Happy. Be Joyous.
Find all of the *good* in life throughout each day.
Live the life of your desires breath by breath,
feeling by feeling, step by step.
Find reasons to smile,
feel happy, *feel* joy, *feel* a sense of inner peace.
Practice, practice, practice all of these actions
each and every day.

1

BEING CREATIVE

Each and every one of us is especially creative in some way or another. Sometimes we believe that our talents have yet to be discovered. And, that may be true. We may not recognize our natural creative talents. An easy daily indulgence in activities that are really fun and interesting uplifts our sense of well-being. The most fun and interesting activities are the source of our natural creativity.

To further expand on our natural creativity, think about how to be creative in a sharing way, with whatever brings feelings of great pleasure. Sharing our creativity enhances the fun of creating, and brings joy to others as they receive the creation. Worry not about who will and won't like the shared creations. None of that matters. Only the joy that any creation brings is what matters.

Practicing activities that feel like fun and that make us smile, even a little, are among the best ways known for taking good care of ourselves, and for improving our quality of life. They are the avenues that connect us with our Inner-Child.

They are the activities that bring us happiness, a sense of quiet peace to calm our nerves, and even joy to our sense of well-being.

Everyone has natural creative talents. Everyone.
Expressing our natural creativity
supports our well-being.
Being creative fosters a sense of purpose deep inside us.
Practicing our natural creativity uplifts our feelings.

Practicing our creative talents is a good way for replacing any unwanted feelings with feelings of comfort and harmony. Whatever our discontent, be it sadness, loneliness, lack of a purposeful direction, or something else, all can be relieved by us in a natural way. We can each uplift our feelings by connecting with and practicing our natural creative talents. Frequent practice of joy-giving activities promotes our self-confidence and helps us to be all that we are capable of being. We could even be surprised by our abilities, as we allow ourselves an unleashed freedom to be creative. This is the essence of our Inner-Child coming out to play. **Enjoying the actions of an activity with our senses and our feelings takes us into a timeless dimension of peace and happiness, to a place where our emotions can heal.** Emotional barriers are diminished when we practice our natural creative talents. These barriers are steeped in the thoughts of an excuse. A common excuse sounds like, "I can't do that because . . . ." This type of mental self-programming is what prevents us from living the life that we desire and dream of.

Carving out just a portion of each day for practicing what we most enjoy can carry us through additional hours of feeling the glow of happiness and joy. The more time we spend doing what we enjoy, the better our outlook on life. Barriers become smaller and appear at less frequent intervals. The more time we can spend being timelessly happy each day, the less space there is for self-defeating thoughts to upset our joy.

Being naturally creative encompasses all sorts of talents beyond drawing, painting, handcrafts, dancing, playing musical instruments, sewing, gardening, cutting and pasting. Being naturally creative comes from tuning in with our imagination and expressing our thoughts and feelings in an externally visible way. Just solving puzzles brings out natural creativity. Building a structure with materials of different shapes is another outlet for creativity. The structure could be a high rise art form, a collage for hanging on the wall, a free moving mobile, a table arrangement. It could be assembled with toy blocks or items collected from a nature walk, or with items from around the house. If the activity brings simple joy into our lives, we're being creative. This is what playtime is all about for young children. We still have it within us to create with the happy abandonment of our early childhood. Our Inner-Child remains within us throughout our lives.

This part of our inner-being is a source of love, happiness, joy, good-will, and any sense of innocence that comes to mind.

Practicing activities of creativity either indoors or out in nature bolsters our sense of well-being. The action of being creative improves our feelings of self-worth. We gain a sense of dignity and the feeling that maybe we do have a purpose in life, that we are needed and valued by others for our part in weaving the fabric-of-life. Others may want to share in our creative talents as they are awed and inspired by them in various ways. This is a great way to be a role-model. Meanwhile, we are enjoying ourselves by practicing our creative activities. Pleasing ourselves is an act of self-care. Self-care is an act of kindness that we direct toward ourselves. It promotes our sense of well-being.

Engage in the activities that you enjoy as often as possible. If you can't think of anything to do, go back to the earliest creative fun activities from your childhood memories, and revisit the activity that you most enjoyed. Think forward through the years. Recall the happy times from your childhood until you come to an activity that clicks with you now. The good memories will always be there for you to choose from. Try out as many activities as you'd like. For me, finger painting first jumped to mind, and cutting out snowflakes, playing with my tabby cat (who at least once actually let me dress her in doll clothes and ever so briefly rode in the doll carriage), digging to China in a vacant lot with the neighborhood kids, pretend-playing adult role models, playing games of all sorts, play-cooking special dishes, and the memories keep on coming. Activities from memories of early childhood can be up-dated to fit current age-appropriate forms. Your Inner-Child is always with you, yearning for some fun activity and to play in some way. Do what brings you joy in a socially acceptable way. Fill the days of your life as creatively as possible. **It could be that living the life of your dreams and desires is as simple as expressing your natural creative talents in a way that brings happiness to you and shining that happiness out to others.**

Practicing your natural creative
talents is life-supporting.
Be Happy. Be Joyous.
Start by doing this for your self-care,
for your sense of well-being.
Shine your happiness out into the world around you.

2

CHOOSING VALUES FOR GUIDANCE

This tool supports our best outcome decisions. It answers the questions of what action to take and what activity to engage in for bringing the happiness and joy we imagine for ourselves. To begin, we identify distinct integrity values to live by as a daily guide. It's best to choose values that resonate with our unique and individual deep inner being.

Two important values are honesty and self-care:

<u>Honesty</u>
Being honest with ourselves transfers naturally into being honest with others. This will eliminate the need for lying, stealing, and any other form of related harmful behavior that we direct toward ourselves and others. **Being honest no matter what, is a wonderful value to model for everyone.**

Some people have practiced dishonesty for so long, that they have lost the frame-of-reference for thinking, speaking, and acting honestly. In comparison, life is easier and so much richer in quality when we conduct ourselves with actions of the highest integrity possible.

Whether actions are honest or dishonest, they will always boomerang and come back around to the sender in a reflection of what was sent out. Know that the return effect of the boomerang is in direct proportion to whatever action is sent out into relationship interactions and to society in general. This is one of the basic laws of physics. It is also good to know that our thoughts are made up of the same vibrational energy as physical actions. They express as different wavelengths, yet it is all made of the same energy vibrations. And energy vibrations are scientifically measurable. They are tangible. A thought vibration can be measured. The important point is that every thought shoots out into the universe and impacts us just as physical actions impact us.

That said, it is important to be ever mindful of our thoughts. Thoughts really are actions. The same is true for spoken and written messages. Being mindful of our thoughts means sending out only what we want coming back to us. We each have free-will to design our lives by however we choose to think and act. This exercise invites us to investigate possible options by asking and then feeling from our heart-center: "How do I envision my life unfolding?" What is the deep driving force of what really matters, for bringing happiness and joy into our daily lives? Digging deep within, some may think that the most popular answer is about having a certain quantity or quality of material *things*. Instead, good relationships are the favored option. People will often give up riches for relationships.

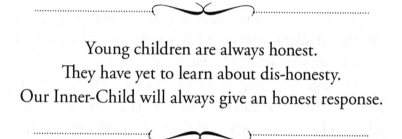

Young children are always honest.
They have yet to learn about dis-honesty.
Our Inner-Child will always give an honest response.

<u>Self Care</u>
When we care about our welfare in body, mind and emotions, we naturally start caring about the welfare of others in healthy ways. We all have the same deep inner desires to be loved, cared about, receive good quality attention, to be respected, appreciated, acknowledged, accepted and included by others. It is best to practice these qualities first on ourselves.

We are worthy and deserving of truly loving ourselves and of liking ourselves just as we are, no matter what happens in life. It is important to care about our well-being, and to give ourselves the attention that we need each day. Always, we must respect ourselves for who we are, meet our needs, monitor our boundaries, and so on. Learn to appreciate all that is good, loving, and kind about our uniquely individual way of being human. Privately acknowledge successes in learning and efforts that take us forward through life. It is so very important to accept ourselves as we are today, and to really enjoy the things that we like about ourselves.

This exercise is a personal journey for rekindling our trust and joy in ourselves.

As we invite relationships with others into our lives, we can apply our feelings of renewed inner trust and joy in life. In return, we'll experience willingness from others to include us in their lives. We receive what we give out into our daily lives. The skills we learn while practicing relationship development with ourselves just naturally carry over into our external relationships.

To experience the best quality of external relationship results, we first need to have a healthy and stable

relationship with ourselves. Being our own best friend is a key element in the quality of our overall happiness in life.

"Be kind to yourself and to others."
This is an essential practice for bringing harmony and peace into all life on Earth.
"Be kind to yourself and to others."
Being kind to one another transcends all differences of race, language, culture, beliefs, nationality, age, ability, every aspect of life.
"Be kind to yourself and to others."
No training or education is required. No discussion is needed to explain how to be kind; being kind comes from our heart-felt feelings.
"Be kind to yourself and to others."

"Be kind to yourself and to others" is a good saying to keep in mind each day. It could bring about consistently happy changes in relationship interactions. Kindness is magical.

Start Your Self-Care Journey by Being Kind to Yourself.

You say that that being kind is easier said than done?
I say: Practice, practice, practice.

Support yourself in situations when you would have typically reprimanded yourself for making an error. Instead, tell yourself that it's okay, the error can be corrected. Tell yourself that you know the error was unintentional, and so on. Nurture yourself. Help yourself recover from the error and move on with your day in a happy state-of-mind.

Harsh punishment is never effective. This includes self-punishment. I believe that we all have that sense of that knowingness deep within our being. Let's start re-thinking our approach to how we live our lives. Self-care is a good place to start.

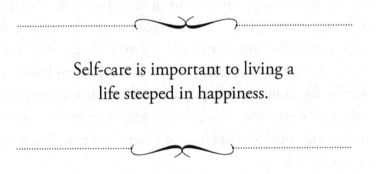

Self-care is important to living a
life steeped in happiness.

Practice values that resonate with you. Treat yourself in a way that brings you peace and a sense of well-being. Then in an open-hearted and caring way, project out to others that same treatment. Remember that we are all the same at our core of emotions. Remember that we all have the same emotional needs and desires for living a life of peace, safety, of being treated with kindness, to be loved and nurtured and accepted without judgment. Even though we are each uniquely individual beings, we all share this aspect of human nature.

3

COMMUNE WITH NATURE FOR EMOTIONAL HEALING

For this next tool put away your phone, if possible. You are more important right now than anyone or anything else that is going on. The world will wait for you to take this time in nature for your self care. This is a relationship building exercise for building community, a kinship, a connection with the many different ways that nature serves our needs with sights, sounds, sensations of touch, and materials used for our daily lives.

Communing with Nature is the Great Emotional Healer. Being outdoors in the natural environment is where plants are growing, where bugs, birds, and animals of all sorts perform a symphony celebrating daily life. It's a place where water flows, ever-changing, as it also calmly reflects the world around it. So much life activity is happening all at once. Go out your door and smell the smells of living plants, listen to the sounds of nature, hear the song of leaves as they flutter to the beat of soft wind blowing against them. Now feel the movement of a breeze, scented by nature, blowing across your skin and through your hair. Check in with your feelings, your emotions about each of these sensations. How does nature feel to you? Walk in it at a pace that is comfortable for you to enjoy. Gradually extend the distance you travel through nature as your muscles and stamina strengthen.

The experience of being in nature is enhanced when attending to your breath, inhalations and exhalations, and to your emotions. How are you feeling as you take each step and see the sights, hear the sounds, and smell the smells? Talk to yourself about what you are sensing. What are your emotional reactions? Enjoy yourself. Laugh at yourself when your reaction surprises you. What else comes through your mind? Be your authentic self when out in Nature. This is a great training ground for learning to reconnect with your Inner-Child.

Nature helps us shed the cloak of social conditioning
that has drawn us away from the
truest sense of our inner-self.

As your reactions, your thoughts, your responses all shift toward greater degrees of self respect, self caring, and self love; they will also be reflected in your outer world of relationships and activities of daily living. Magical moments like that will occur more and more often, even when away from nature, bringing an easier flow to daily activities. And that is a wonderful way of living. It's what we are all seeking and searching for: that inner sense of joy, of well-being, happiness, security, and that wonderful indescribable feeling of love –unconditional love flowing in and then radiating out from within our heart-center. Time spent in a natural environment enhances all of these wonderful changes in our lives. It's what comes from the magical moments experienced in out in nature.

There is also a profound silence found in nature. When tromping through a forest, on a mountain trail, beside a lake, or out in an open area, pause. Stand completely still and listen. This is when complete silence can be experienced. It's powerful. It's calming. It's energizing. Silence in nature is this and more. It is there for each individual to uniquely describe the experience. It is something worth experiencing. Sometimes the wind is blowing, and all one can hear is the wind. This is a variation on silence. Check in with the feelings that the sound of a steady wind brings.

Nature can be uplifting for our Inner-Child's sense of wonder and delight. Somehow, make a point to carve out some of each day, to get in touch with the gentleness of nature, to rejuvenate, and to bring our sense of self into a feeling of peace. The more we are out in nature, the more we learn about plants and animals, birds and insects, and the rhythms of nature. It is a place of simple honesty. The always interesting environment varies by elevation and latitude. Maybe you've heard the term "the wonders of nature." The wonders are out there, waiting for individual discovery.

Remember: Porch sitting counts as being out in nature. It has not gone out of style. And, it's free. Turn off your phone and look up at the sky. Watch the clouds as they change form. Look around at life as the world passes by your view. Listen to the sounds of nature. Feel the air movement on your skin. Smell the smells of newly cut grass, the smell of all plants, especially the flowers. Nature is one of the greatest shows on Earth. Enjoy it.

Breath Exercise 1 Mindful Breath of Life

As often as possible throughout each day pause and notice how you feel –in your gut, in your heart, in your head, in your muscles. Just observe.

Next, breathe in as you say to yourself one (1) to four (4) words of life values that are meaningful for you. Use words that bring a sense of love, joy, and happiness that uplift you.

Pause your breath, and then fully exhale saying to yourself words of release and relief that are meaningful to you. These are words that release tension and bring peace, good feelings and joy.

Notice how you feel. Then, return to your activity of daily living.

Over time, try out different words
till hitting upon words
that really move your inner feelings
from tension to feeling good
by the end of the exhale.
Go for words that are very personal to you.
Some word examples are: Love, Healing, Peace,
Joy, Release, Allow, Faith, Receive, Giving,
Bliss, Harmony, Trust, Patience, Patient, Kind,
Safe, Protected, Agree, Support, Courage.

– This exercise helps with pain relief for both physical and emotional distress.

– Breathe in Peace, Love, Harmony, Balance, Perfect Health.

– Breathe out Release, Stress, Anger, Resentment, Blame, Judgment, Fear.

– And, breathe out Love, Kindness, Community.

– Pause before the next inhalation and notice the level of muscle relaxation.

– Take another mindful breath and release even more tension.

This exercise is safe to practice while driving and riding vehicles. Years ago, it helped keep my mind focused and energy level elevated, while motorcycle touring hour after hour along straight stretches of highway on those six and seven to eight hundred mile days.

4

Letting Go of Excuses

During my 20s, I mostly lived in a personal bubble. Sometimes I read magazines and newspapers, mostly books, lots of books. Years went by without having a television for news, and often I lived without a telephone. Pay phones were abundant for the occasional phone call. Some news came through on the car radio. It was a time when computers were all connected to a main-frame. Printed circuit boards were in the early stages of development. Leisure time was rich with travel experiences, movies at the theatre, live entertainment, and outdoor activities, all enjoyed at a more relaxed pace than most people get to experience today.

Even though life went along at a slower pace, it went along. Weather satellites didn't exist. High flying airplanes and weather balloons sent back upper atmosphere information. To forecast weather, I watched the sky, noted the wind, the clouds, temperatures, and smells in the air. Weather observation can be a fun pastime. Meanwhile, I missed large chunks of years and years of social and political news details, catching only the highlights. And, that was easily enough exposure to pass a general history exam. Looking back, my life was mostly peaceful, and filled with joy; whether living in a small town, a resort community, or a metropolis. It was a life of work, marriage, family, friends, outdoor recreation, hobbies; a simple life with variety provided through ever-constant changes (a rare oxymoron exception). Change is our only constant in life.

The point here is that missing blow-by-blow social and political news had no direct impact on my daily life. Knowing or not knowing the details of current news made no difference in my daily decisions. This is an important distinction to ponder and explore, as we feel the feelings of our reactions, of our considerations, of our investigative thoughts about the world around us. Attending to just the important points of daily news can be enough. The remaining majority of each day can be filled with focusing on living in a way that supports the highest quality of life for ourselves.

Like a young child, daily decisions can be made based upon our feelings.

Our daily lives are personal and exist within a realm that is separate and independent of the social and political world around us.

Practice making decisions based upon your personal inner-guidance and not in reaction to global activities or how friends and neighbors are living their lives.

Other helpful news to remember is that:

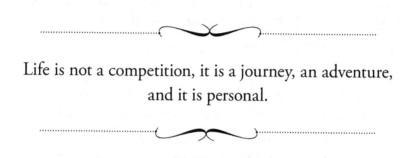

Life is not a competition, it is a journey, an adventure, and it is personal.

Yes, whole-heartedly be involved in global activities from a kind and respectful approach, in a life-supporting approach. Join in when it is your choice to take helpful, supportive action -not when involvement comes from an impulsive reaction of resistance steeped in fear. Follow your inner guidance to seek peace and joy.

Trust your feelings to take you in the
direction of your highest vision for life.
It matters not what other people think
about your activities and decisions.
Follow the wise guidance of *your* Inner-Child,
and forge your personalized life path.
No excuses allowed.

Through practice, you will arrive at every honestly heart-centered vision of your desires. When you do, you will see and know that there is always more to seek, taking you ever higher into the realms of joy and peace within your being. Keep on keeping on. Life is good and keeps getting better. Go forward with love and good-will in your heart-centered feelings. Live with the feeling of open-hearted kindness toward life. Embrace life. Enjoy yourself. No barriers or limitations from excuses allowed. Just live with an open heart in love-filled joy as often as possible.

5

THE VALUE OF LIVING A GOOD LIFE

1. *The value of standing tall (physically).*
2. *The value of smiling, even when alone.*
3. *The value of thinking good thoughts, all of the time.*
4. *The value of kindness toward yourself and others.*
5. *The value of day-dreaming, of visualizing the life of your dreams.*
6. *The value of being out in nature,* of immersing yourself in the sights, sounds, smells, the feel of clean air from a breeze or even stronger wind against your face and body. This is a lot of incoming energy. It is more nurturing for feeling a sense of inner-peace, than the high excitement of city energy. The sublime energy of nature is every bit as exciting and uplifting as city energy, but offers a lower stress level. Please investigate with an open mind the experience of both sides presented. Only good can come from expanding our horizons.
7. *The value of good tasting and nutritious food.* Nutritious food is naturally grown and sourced for eating directly

from the earth. Nutritious food fuels our bodies and promotes health. In comparison, processed foods have little to no nutritional value. Processed foods break down our bodies and create entry points for diseases to root and grow; thus, diminishing our daily activity abilities. What quality of life do you choose? How vibrantly alive do you choose to feel?

8. *The value of movement, both mental movement and physical movement.* Keep on moving on. Keep your youthful curiosity alive and active. Learn new things about life. There is always something new to learn. Also, keep your body moving throughout each day. When you sit long enough and often enough, your ability to walk will eventually disappear. Keep those muscles and joints in good operating condition, so they can serve you throughout your life.

9. *The value of rhythm in rest and activity.* Live life in a balanced rhythm of adequate rest and measured activity, to increase harmony in daily life activities. This is a value that especially resonates with your Inner-Child. A balance of rest and activity provides good energy for enjoying activities. Measured activities are accomplished with greater ease when supported by a rested feeling of calm inner peace. Pace yourself. Rest when tired. Get going again physically and mentally when rested. It's a nice balance for optimizing our health and creativity.

10. *The value of releasing resistance.* Release what you are resisting. Allow life to flow without your constant efforts to control everything. Take care of your personal needs and desires in a kind and thoughtful

way. By relaxing your inner tension, your resistance to life events releases with a natural ease. Life can flow without your direct involvement in external affairs. The need to always be right is a form of resistance that obstructs the natural flow of life. Stand back and observe with interest, the unfolding of life events. The variations that work out well may surprise you, and even change your thoughts in a good way. I have long said that there are at least six different ways to do everything imaginable, and have the same result.

11. *The value of giving and receiving.* Both equally important, this is where joy excels. Who knew life could be so good, and so easy? And free of charge, no money or objects are required to give and to receive. Examples are: Kindness – Smiles – Hugs – Kisses – Helping Hand – Compliment – Thoughts of Good-Will, plus any other gestures of giving and receiving that come to mind.

For living a good life, meld your inner
needs into your outer life.
Do this with as much kindness,
care, and respect for yourself
and for others that you can give.
Just do your best in any given moment.
And Practice, practice, practice.

Notice all of the ways that life actually gets better each day. It's in the details. Notice the small things, like breathing. Breath awareness is a good place to begin reigning in our thoughts so that we can notice the details of daily life. Observing our breath moving in and out reminds us that without breathing, we would not be reading this book. Observing our breath is a good activity for standing in line, waiting at a traffic light, while watching life activities going on around you, and while just listening and not thinking.

Meanwhile, when thoughts are flowing, think about and appreciate all of the body parts that allow our senses to function, our bodies to move as we desire, Think about and appreciate the endless series of ingenuity and craftsmanship the goes into creating the vehicle you get around in, the clothes you wear, and every convenience in your life. Break each convenience item down into all of the contributing factors. Surprisingly, every thread followed to the beginning of an end product will start from resources provided by our planet. When considering life from these perspectives, there is great value in living a good life. The details are all worth appreciating.

Support for living a good life is found in some easy things to notice about each day:

Feelings. Attend to your feelings. Follow the gift of your inner-guidance. Go with what feels good. Remember that you can change your mind as often as needed to support your well-being and the well-being of others.

Explore for yourself the rhythm of routine versus chaos.
Example: Is routine boring? Is chaos exciting? Is routine soothing, peaceful? Is chaos stressful?

Explore for yourself the evidence of love versus fear. Are your actions steeped in love or in fear?

Thoughts of your highest vision for life. This is something to always keep in mind.

Feeling Good. Explore what that means to you.

Spinal alignment and energy flow are essential. Stand or sit tall, stretching the top of your spine toward the sky while stretching the lower end of your spine toward the earth. This stretch will help hold your head up, pull your shoulders back, your abdomen and stomach will pull in, and your chest expands allowing greater air exchange. All of this is happening together with surprising ease.

More on feelings, our guiding compass. Go for the good feelings. Let the not-so-good feelings fade away. Feelings work with our thoughts. Thoughts produce feelings, and vice versa. Think thoughts that support the highest vision of life. This heart-centered feel-good way of being came to us naturally as young children. For the best quality of life, it would be worth regenerating that feeling of joy and delight in life –for every day of our life.

Strive to become best friends with your Inner-Child.

Laughter really is the best medicine.
Seek joy.
Laugh with joy at the simple delights of life.
At least smile for starters.
That joy is inside you, and everyone.

6

Exploring Childhood

Life is *magical* as seen through the eyes of wonder and joy. No need to lament childhood. That young child you recall still lives inside you. Allow your Inner-Child to laugh and to play as you recall the times of expressing yourself with reckless abandon, and feeling only joy in your play activities.

Zero judgment toward ourselves and the world around us was the key element in all of that joy. As young children, we just allowed each day to unfold in a natural way. We had no schedules or agendas. We had completely forgotten about the previous day. All days were the same in our minds. The rhythm of day and night and back to day was simply a continuous flow, of one moment melding into the next moment. We had no concept of time that brings us through yesterday, today and tomorrow. This concept of time can really skew our *sense of being* in the present moment. If we have forgotten about yesterday and not planned an itinerary for tomorrow, all we have left is today. Distill today down into this present moment. If the present moment is all that we have, where is there space for holding resentment and judgment?

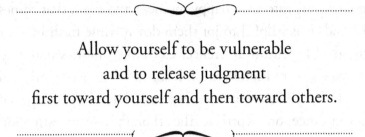

Allow yourself to be vulnerable
and to release judgment
first toward yourself and then toward others.

Releasing judgment is a worthy challenge that takes mindful and continued practice. Start by feeling your emotions; and, choosing each time to go with the ones that fuel kindness and good-will. Remember that we are each only responsible for our own thoughts and actions. It may also be helpful to remember that we are always serving as role-models as we go through our daily activities. We influence others just by being ourselves. Are your words and actions representing your highest vision of life?

Take a look at young childhood, again. We interacted in life events without any feelings of judgment. When angered or upset we quickly let the incident go (back into the nothingness from which it came) to focus on the next thing that sparked our attention. Our thoughts never went back to the cause of whatever upset us. We had forgotten about it and moved on to the next ever-unfolding events in our life. Try applying this exercise for the remainder of today. Then, try it again tomorrow and every day after that. Practice, practice, and practice.

Also, weigh-in on the happy memories in your life. Model your daily activities in the spirit of what has made you happy throughout your life. Think back to the earliest times of happiness and joy in your childhood. Go forward through time tapping into each happy moment and event that comes to mind. It is helpful to jot them down while fresh in your thoughts, for future reference. Certain memories may pop into your inner-vision later on. If so, add them to the original notations. This recent memory may have been a special circumstance, one worth further thought and investigation into your feelings about it then, and your feelings now.

Remember that this is a personal journey. We each have a one-of-a-kind version of our life, as viewed through our unique perception and memory log. My sister, mother, and I would gather and talk about past family events. We each recited our own recollection of the occasions, and the three versions were always presented somewhat differently. Some versions even sounded like they came from a separate rather than the same household. This happened enough times to know that each life-journey is personal and unique. Knowing that we each have a personal and unique perception of life events is another reason to forgo judgment of anyone's behavior. Support what is kind, and uplifting. Send thoughts of good-will instead of judgment.

Delve into your personal past, drawing visions from your earliest memories. These are the least polluted memories, before social structuring of your personality took dominance and overshadowed your Inner-Child.

7

LIFE ON THE ROAD

As we plow through the trials and tribulations of this life, something remarkable happens on a regular basis. We experience *change* in every form imaginable. Change happens all day every day. It happens as we learn what we need to know, about how to live life in the most happy and enjoyable ways possible. Change could be called the "pulse" of life, the "beat and the pause" of experiencing life on Earth. Change influences, stirs, and excites all of life on Earth, in Earth and above Earth, as it all expands and contracts in harmony, through the breath and the beat of life.

Imagine the different ways that all of life experiences change, seeming to be in constant motion. The changes that we each experience individually throughout our lifetime, the happy, the sad, and indifferent, are all a natural part of living life on Earth. This is the operating condition of life. Life in all its forms is dynamic and in constant rhythmic motion. Change dominates, as the pauses in motion are brief. There is a law in physics having to do with homeostasis that demonstrates this pulse and pause of life. We may all want a steady and unchanging life experience, but change is our life energy. Embrace change with enthusiastic child-like awe and wonder, for whatever may be coming next along our road of life. Life really is an adventure.

As we look around in nature, imagine how a beautiful gentle river may feel when inundated with flood water roiling through its course, ripping and tearing at everything in its path. This is change for the river. And after the flood, the river recovers, flowing calmly. It becomes beautiful again, until the next inevitable flood, or maybe an earthquake or a tornado shapes the next change in the scenery and the course of the river. This isn't some tragedy. It's part of the dynamics of how our planet breathes, through the pulses and the pauses. Usually it's external forces that spark change into motion. This example runs true in every area and category of life, ourselves included.

We humans are similar to the qualities of Earth when exploring the subject of change. The differences are mostly in scale and types of changes. This is the case for each person, as we are uniquely individual in our life-changing experiences. Change is at the core of our way of living. Each day is different from any other day. Even when we think that we are doing the same things in the same way day in and day out, there are differences each day that make it unique. Check on this concept, to know the truth of it for yourself. Compare all of the details of yesterday and today with tomorrow.

This road of life we travel is full of surprises as we go along our way. In some way there is always an element of good in every situation and event. It is helpful to find the goodness, even if it is a life lesson. Instead of resisting change, try embracing change. Welcome change. Go forward through each day with feelings of love and gratitude in your heart-center, for the privilege of being a part of this life. Life can be physically, intellectually, and emotionally challenging. And, it is equally a wonder-filled journey. Relax into life changes. Look forward to what is around the next turn on your individually unique life-journey.

A way to ease the process of change is to send out thoughts of good-will and well-being for yourself and others as often as possible. Be kind to yourself and to all of life that you encounter throughout each day. Step into the changes presented before you throughout each new day, knowing that you can always change your mind about your decisions. Do this any time a change moves you toward an unwanted direction: Call a halt and change direction.

We *always* have more chances to live a better life than the one we are living today –*always*. Just keep on keeping on toward your highest vision for yourself. Follow your feelings of heart-centered inner guidance about what direction to take. Go for the choices that make you feel good, that make you feel happy with a sense of well-being, and that bring a smile. All will be okay.

Every change in direction will work out even better than originally envisioned. Life will introduce more happy surprises along the way than sad ones. Look for the happy ones. Enjoy yourself and your daily life. Make the best of every situation. It is all good. More chances and opportunities are just ahead on your path. Greet them with enthusiastic expectation and good-will. Young children are quite naturally enthusiastic in their exploration of each new day. **That young child still lives within your feelings. Trust your feelings. They come from your inner-wisdom.**

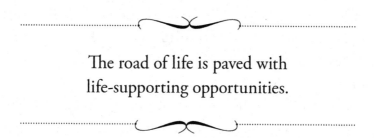

The road of life is paved with
life-supporting opportunities.

8

SOME KEY CONCEPTS

Here are a few key concepts that go very well together:
It is not possible to fail.
We always get more chances.
There is always enough time.
Frantically racing through the day is unnecessary.
Do you see these all together as a working unit of life?

Is there ever a young child who gives a thought to any of these ideas? Can you take yourself back to that time of just being and doing, testing and testing again, succeeding and trying the next challenge? Did time ever matter? Yesterday, today and tomorrow were all the same, flowing as a continuous stream-of-life. We ate when hungry, slept when tired, were active and explored life the rest of the time. There are no rules saying that we cannot take ourselves back to that time and live each day from that state of mind.

It was somewhere near the early days of kindergarten when my son was becoming aware of yesterday, today, and tomorrow. He wrestled with and mixed up these concepts for what seemed like weeks; asking over and over for explanations to clarify *time* in his mind, and in what direction it goes. Sadly, I helped him wash away his sense of timelessness, just so he could be on-time in this modern-day society.

We can hark back to that timeless essence of young childhood as we try-out new ideas that interest us. With that frame of reference, we can go forward into unknown territory without worries and cares for yesterday, today and tomorrow, because we have internal tools of wisdom to guide us. Turning within ourselves, we can listen to the quiet voice of wisdom from our Inner-Child. We can respond to our feelings. By following our inner guidance, we can keep ourselves safe from harm and make choices that enhance our quality of life, step by step. We can act on reminder cues to be patient with ourselves. We can take on new ventures in workable steps. Taking on life changes in big leaps can be avoided. We can sidestep any associated emotional pain and even physical pain from crashes when trying to take giant steps. The best choice is to take smaller steps with small stumbling block possibilities. It is the kinder way to treat ourselves. This slower pace also gives us a chance to gain knowledge and inner strength about our choices. Then later on, with our growing knowledge base, we can explore a larger scope of possibilities by taking some bigger steps. Taking leaps are not recommended, unless they are grounded in a deep inner knowingness that the result(s) will serve and support life.

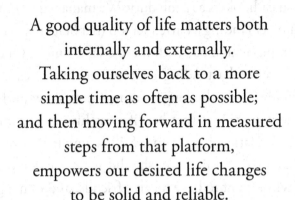

A good quality of life matters both
internally and externally.
Taking ourselves back to a more
simple time as often as possible;
and then moving forward in measured
steps from that platform,
empowers our desired life changes
to be solid and reliable.

One of my memorable counseling clients had lived through a childhood of abusive treatment. An intelligent and good-hearted young woman with a multiple felony record, protected her vulnerability with what she knew so well, with physical violence. During counseling she adopted an increasingly acceptable social presence, taking it step by step. First steps were to no longer wear her FELON belt buckle and the custom engraved brass knuckles, worn as a handy necklace. Outfits became more loose-fitting and less revealing, makeup was lighter. These were boundary stretching challenges that she bravely took on each week, building upon her successful steps. And justifiably, she felt better about herself; her natural beauty was opening up from the inside out. She was smiling and laughing more often. Though, stepping back into a low paying job and having the patience to work up the social ladder was too big of a concession at that time. She could quickly make a month's worth of sales associate wages by working as a barmaid. Most bars in that area required barmaids to also be quasi-hookers as a job duty. We managed to tone that down into her landing a bartender job (her State requirements already in place) at a bar with more civil clientele. Openings for this level of bartending environment were scarce, and she willingly made the longer commute to show-up for her shift. The downside is that her life was historically unstable and full of relationship drama. Still struggling through an emotionally painful lifestyle, she did what she could in her social environment to have reliable friends, and to hang onto enough money for food, rent and other necessities. Though not yet emotionally content, the momentum was swinging toward a healthier lifestyle for herself and her family. She was taking steps forward as she walked the talk of her desires. The next step for this determined young woman was to finish her college program on a more regular basis. She was signed up for classes starting immediately. Additional steps were in the queue. This is a story of success in action. When we are ready to make a change, the doors appear and open as we approach them.

The self-acceptance and forgiveness process the woman in this story was walking through is the same for all of us. It matters not, about the level of living conditions and circumstances, or when and where we start our recovery journey of reconnecting with our Inner-Child. It matters that we start. Connecting through our emotions and feelings with our Inner-Child state-of-mind is a tool that helps us live our lives in greater peace and harmony. Take it easy on yourself as you walk through your life-journey. Remembering these next statements will help build inner strength.

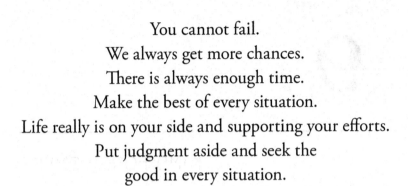

You cannot fail.
We always get more chances.
There is always enough time.
Make the best of every situation.
Life really is on your side and supporting your efforts.
Put judgment aside and seek the
good in every situation.

Remember to make every moment count toward living the life of your heart-felt desires. Throughout the day, pause and observe your breath, the air moving in and out. Relax into your breathing and allow a smile of relief. Can you feel this in your heart-center? Ask inwardly for your Inner-Child guidance and direction on your life-path. Then, follow your thoughts and feelings for taking the next action step. Remember to choose the outcome visions that make you feel genuinely good inside. Keep on keeping on.

9

KIND FORGIVENESS

To forgive ourselves and to forgive others is an important key in living the life of our dreams. As we move toward our highest visions, we come to understand that everything is forgivable –everything. Forgive and ask to be forgiven. Then, that is the end of it. Go forward and move on with your life. Let go of feeling any negative emotions toward the situation and toward anyone involved. Continuing to be upset about it just keeps anger fueled and burning. Why would anyone want to live with the emotionally harmful feelings of unforgiveness? No good or happiness can come of it –ever.

Meanwhile, the sordid thoughts of unforgiveness eventually cause physical ailments throughout the body. Who would want to wish physical pain and suffering upon themselves, on top of the already existing emotional pain? That makes no good sense, for any reason. Forgiveness is not about accepting or justifying an action or situation. It is an act of compassionate understanding, a releasing of blame. A relationship may or may not be mended when we forgive others. Whether reconciled or not, forgive yourself and forgive others. Do this for your own well-being.

Then, move on with a feeling of peace in your heart-center. Send thoughts of good-will toward others who you have forgiven. This helps to reconcile and reinforce the forgiving. Only goodness for yourself and everyone involved can come of these actions. Peace is created to replace anger and bitterness. The peace you feel within yourself is the most important outcome, from having forgiven all who were involved. I have long said that if we knew better deep within us, not just an intellectual knowing, that we would do better. We all eventually get to that more desirable place of knowing. In the meantime, forgive the human errors along the way.

Go back again to viewing the ways of being a young child: Notice that there is never a time of unforgiveness in early childhood; hence, no emotional pain. It's just another day of joy and happiness. Unforgiveness is a learned behavior that is emotionally harmful. It fuels emotional pain in us, first when not forgiving our own anger, and then by not forgiving others who have bruised our beliefs and feelings. Release the anger and the ego justification. Your Inner-Child will thank you.

There are always more chances to complete a life lesson in a loving, kind, and compassionate manner. Know that the lesson will keep coming up in your life (in a stronger way each time) until you do get it completed in the most loving, kind and compassionate way. So ease that process by first forgiving yourself and then by forgiving others.

Go forward from where you are to the next moment of life-adventure. The more closely we follow our quiet inner guidance from thoughts and feelings, the easier the lessons. As more heart-felt decisions are made, the easier the path when the lessons are more challenging. Remember to feel your feelings and check in with yourself about what decision will make you feel the happiest. If you are happy, chances are those around you will also be happy. Distill down the situation through all of the trappings and get to the core of what is going on. Act from that position.

When I am in a state of dis-ease and not living in my higher integrity, eating an unhealthy diet, engaging in activities that do not serve and support life, and when not staying focused on my highest thoughts and visions, my sleep is interrupted with nightmares reminding me of my daily discontent. The lesson? I have choices during the day about how to conduct my moment to moment thoughts and actions. The more kindness and lack of judgment I express toward myself and others, the easier the day flows and the sweeter the nighttime dreams.

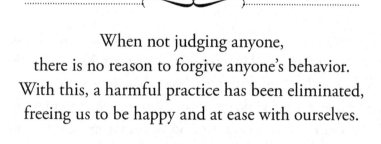

When not judging anyone,
there is no reason to forgive anyone's behavior.
With this, a harmful practice has been eliminated,
freeing us to be happy and at ease with ourselves.

It is a helpful practice to release all jealousy, blame, shame, grievances, regrets and guilt. Stop complaining. And then, notice how much smoother and easier your life flows throughout each day. Go back to that young childhood state-of-mind, where you only wanted to feel good. Listen to and feel that part of yourself. Your Inner-Child is always there to serve your needs and sooth your emotions.

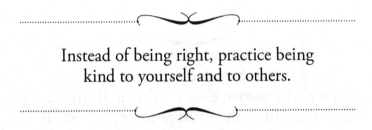

Instead of being right, practice being
kind to yourself and to others.

Relax and take some time to observe your breath going in and out.

Forgive yourself for everything.

Give up judgment of yourself and others. Judgment is unnecessary and harmful.

Make decisions based upon your emotions, your gut feelings, your heart feelings.

Accept yourself as being the best version of you, the one who is always improving the version.

Support yourself with nurturing words when you believe that you have made a mistake.

Tell yourself that it is okay. We always get more chances. Then move on with the day.

"No one is so bereaved, so miserable, that he cannot find someone else . . . who needs friendship, understanding, and courage more than he. The unselfish effort to bring cheer to others will be the beginning of a happier life for ourselves."
–Helen Keller

Be kind to yourself and to others.

10

THOUGHTS – FEELINGS – DECISIONS – DIRECTION

Create thoughts and actions of fairness and goodness toward yourself and toward others.

Keep practicing your desires and dreams. Practice always pays off.

We always get what we desire and dream of in the most heart-felt way.

We reach our goals as we take daily steps through the decisions we make.

Every moment presents a decision about
what direction to take with our life.

Please attend to your life breath by breath, moment
by moment, to help quiet your thoughts.

Pointed focus on our breathing takes us to
the quiet place of our Inner-Child.

Magical moments of life happen when we are
feeling at peace and calmly quiet deep inside.

A happy life calls for focused attention to our
feelings, and the decisions we make based them.

Desires and dreams are fulfilled all along our
life-path. Enjoy each moment of the journey.

The details of our highest visions will shift and
change along the way –all for our highest good.

Exercise:

1. Write or type your thoughts as they come to mind, as a form of very informal journaling.

2. Writing thoughts when they pop into your mind relieves you of constantly repeating thoughts, to keep them in your short-term memory.

3. Routinely categorize your thoughts according to when you feel the need to act on each one. Organizing daily would help to keep the exercise manageable. The importance of your various thoughts will change over the passing days, weeks, months, years. Keep an historical log as a tracking reference, and for noticing any patterns that are revealed. Attend to patterns especially, to ensure that they align with your highest visions for yourself.

Organized by importance for taking action. List your thoughts under the sample categories:

today	his month
tomorrow	winter, spring, summer, fall
this week	next year
next week	someday

4. Review your thoughts log at the end of each day. Then release those thoughts from your mind and enjoy restful and peaceful sleep.

5. This easy mind-clearing aide also helps train us for a more organized way of handling daily activities.

Have fun with this exercise, and enjoy it. It is a personalized puzzle of your life.

11

Innocent Trust And Kindness

When we wanted something as a young child, no thought was ever given to an alternative outcome. We wanted what we wanted and expected to get it -now. That often works for infants and toddlers. Getting what we want later in life, especially getting it when we want it is less assured. One aspect of that desire is simple: Life complications and disappointments happen more often when we doubt our abilities and the validity of our desires, when we lose focus on our highest visions for ourselves, and when we don't trust ourselves.

Just think about what you do want and go for it.
Apply your natural talents toward that end goal.
If you keep your thoughts and inner vision
focused on your desired outcome,
it will happen.

Trust yourself. Trust your feelings. Trust your thoughts, the ones that make you feel good inside, the thoughts that bring a smile, that bring you peace and joy deep inside your being. It is true that we need to keep practicing the techniques and tools offered in this book, to perfect the path and the outcome of our desires. The *what if this or that* thoughts that creep into our minds are the ruts and bumps in our path. These are the destructive thoughts that break down our dreams and desires, and that undermine our highest visions. They bring a second-rate often upsetting outcome, and clearly not the outcome we had hoped for and envisioned for ourselves.

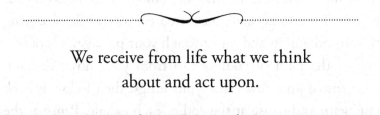

We receive from life what we think
about and act upon.

- Stop hoping for a desired outcome while allowing underlying thoughts of sabotage.
- Start thinking, seeing and feeling yourself living that dreamed-of desire. Then do it.
- Go for your heart-felt desires as an innocent child would go for a target. A child always makes a focused straight beeline toward the object of desire. Be that same way with your dreams and desires.
- With high integrity, take the easiest path possible and enjoy your daily life-journey.

- The more pure that you can keep your dreams and desires for your personal journey, by thinking and envisioning all of the details of your perfect outcome, the closer you'll come to fulfilling that exact vision.

Your Inner-Child, has only your best interest at heart, and desires that your highest vision comes true for you. Stay with the best vision of your dreams and desires. Feel the feel-good feelings in your heart and other muscles when practicing the feelings of your highest visions. Stay with those feelings and keep going in that direction.

When life slams you from the external forces of family, work and social interactions, take a moment to focus on your breath. Take some slow, measured breaths while observing the air moving in and out through your passageways of life. Follow the path of your breath from your nose, through your throat and down into your lungs; then follow it back out again and pause at the end of each exhale. Pause at the end of each inhale.

Now, turn your attention back to your view of the immediate social interaction. What is the kindest reaction that supports yourself, for your best feelings about the situation? Take that action without delay. Being kind to yourself sends kindness as a message to the world. In essence, you are sending a reaction of kindness to the situation while being kind and loving toward yourself. This is a win-win situation.

Always give outwardly what you want to receive. Feel it for yourself first and then express that feeling outwardly. All will be resolved in the best way possible by using this technique. This is how your Inner-Child charms you into getting whatever you desire. It's a tried and true tool for living a good life.

Remember to be genuine and truthful so this technique/ tool works in a lasting way. Be kind and gentle with yourself. You deserve the best and most caring treatment. Like yourself. Love yourself. We are each at our core a deeply loving nonjudgmental child. Reveal that Inner-Child to yourself and the results will just naturally spill out into your daily life events and situations. No extra effort is needed to live a life of feeling good inside. Feeling good, feeling joy is your natural way of being. All that is unwanted will fall away from lack of attention, back into the nothingness from which it came.

12

OUR LIFE IS OUR SOLE RESPONSIBILITY

No one has ever changed another person through force or through punishment who did not agree and allow a change to happen. We all change our way of thinking and our way of being by our own design, by our own desires and decisions. Even behavior changes made to survive in the most adverse conditions can be remedied to reveal the true nature of a person. Our Inner-Child is very determined, always seeking happiness, joy and peace in life. We each decide to be who we are as a human being. Glimpses of our decisions show through in our behavior, in the ways we choose to live our lives. Even if we submerge who we really are, our true sense of self will eventually surface. The secret is in our thoughts. Our thoughts reveal who we are, our moral character

Others can and do influence our ways of thinking and how we conduct our lives. It is our free-will right to decide whether to follow the influence or not. We are all individual in our sense of being; and as individuals, we are in charge of how our lives unfold. How does our Inner-Child react when being diverted from a focused path? There is crying, kicking, even screaming –right? It may be held internally, or expressed outwardly. The resistance to unwanted change is always present.

There are countless ways to live any life situation. Set your sights from deep within your heart-felt desires and head for your destination. Be kind to yourself in choosing your path. This includes your thoughts and actions throughout every day of your life. In this age of having so much information about everything instantly available, finding choices that resonate with your Inner-Child is so easy. When the idea makes your heart ping and your Inner-Child feels delighted –go for it. When the thought of a goal feels good, stay true to the path no matter the obstacles encountered along the way. It is not always an easy path to reach the goals of our dreams and desires. Stretching our comfort zones and feeling resistance from friends and family can cause difficult situations along the way. If the goal is important enough, keep on keeping on. Opportunities will unfold along the way, serving as support to complete the journey.

Sometimes it is best to keep the path of inner journey changes to yourself. As you go along the path of embracing and representing the values that you've been practicing, the folks around you will notice a difference about how you are expressing yourself in relationship interactions. There is no need to explain yourself. Say thank you for the compliments and comments of wonder. Or, reply with a comment along the lines of "It feels pretty good." They will all adjust to and appreciate the "new you."

Try as they may, there is no one who can alter our
life direction in a lasting way without our consent.
Stay true to your heart-felt dreams and desires.

We all have the option of making
personally unique free-will choices.

Make life choices for yourself that
make you feel good inside.

Stay true to your inner sense of knowing
what is best for your life-path.

Absorb the bumps of setbacks along the way,
knowing that we always get more chances –always.

Change the direction of your life
if not feeling good about it
in your heart, your stomach, gut, or muscles.

Keep on keeping on toward your highest visions for living a life filled with happiness, joy, and peace.

The effort to work through obstacles
and fine-tune your highest visions
along your life-path, are well worth the end results.

13

LIVING A BETTER LIFE

We all want to enjoy living a better life. The desires of our ever-present ego are the driving force of always wanting more of everything. There is a secret for living a better life, and ironically the process minimizes our ego. Living a better life starts from inside each of us. When this concept is put into action, our external world keeps getting better and better, and our inner life continues to blossom. **A better life is expressed and experienced by how we feel inside ourselves, about the quality of life outside ourselves.**

What are your thoughts about life? Listen to yourself, to what you are saying to yourself and to others. What are your thoughts about? Are your thoughts and what you are saying taking you along a daily path that represents your deepest and most heart-felt desires and dreams? If not, try flipping every thought and spoken message into what you want instead of what you don't want. Do this with every thought and word, and your life will turn around.

Practice, practice, practice.

This exercise requires that you:

- be honest with yourself.
- are kind to yourself.
- stop judging yourself and life events.
- feel your feelings and react only to the ones that make you feel good inside.

This is how we follow our Inner-Child guidance. Practice first on yourself. Practice until you are relaxed and comfortable with this new way of being with yourself.

Then, find ways to be kind toward others no matter how offensive their behavior. Be kind because you want to be kind, because it makes you feel good to be kind. Hold only these thoughts. Any other thoughts take away from and pollute an action of kindness. The person receiving a mixed message receives it as being an unkind message.

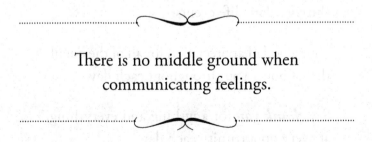

There is no middle ground when communicating feelings.

<u>Some guidelines to remember are:</u>

Conveying thoughts and feelings is a universal language.

The way a person reacts may not reveal the deep level of understanding during an interaction.

The knowingness of truth is always felt during an interaction.

Be genuinely kind to yourself and toward others.

Your Inner-Child responds best to the feel-good feeling of kindness.

Express kindness to yourself and to the world.

A key part of living a better life is by expressing ***gratitude and appreciation*** for everything.

Learn to notice all of the details that carry you through daily life events.

Give a nod of appreciation for all of the details that support you throughout each day.

Say ***thank you*** for anything and everything, at every opportunity each day.

> Say *I appreciate . . . because* (and say why you
> appreciate) as many times possible each day.

Know that life is good and that there is good in every life experience. Sometimes we have to dig deep into our heart-center to see the so-called "silver lining" that is always present in every circumstance and situation. It is also helpful to imagine yourself on the other side of your personal opinion. Try viewing life events with the intention of understand the opposing perspectives.

To varying degrees of intensity, all life events are either a confirmation of being on the right track or as a warning signal to change tracks. This is the nature of our world of duality and polar opposites. Endeavor to see all sides of any situation with the greatest clarity of neutrality and nonjudgement possible. Check in with your Inner-Child guidance by feeling-your-feelings. Consider and weigh outcome possibilities, and then form your action decisions based on what makes you feel the best. Then, act with kindness toward yourself and toward others.

Just as a young child makes a straight-line path toward a desired object, our life journeys unfold in the same manner. Life events help guide our daily direction. Our experiences are directional signals. When we follow the signals, they keep us on our most direct path toward experiencing our deepest, most heart-felt dreams and desires.

It helps to be grateful and to appreciate your life events. It's the life you designed that's unfolding before you. See that your thoughts and decisions match your deepest heart-felt emotions and highest visions for yourself as often as possible.

Your thoughts brought you to this place in your life, and they take you forward through the rest of your life. Today is the tomorrow you were longing for yesterday. Be mindful of your thoughts. Where are they taking you?

This chapter reminded me of an excellent dentist who I had the privilege of assisting. During the four years of employment in that office, he did not miss even a single day of making eye contact and saying thank you to me at the end of the day. That gesture was as distinctly significant, as it was a simple and genuine gesture of kindness and appreciation. Saying thank you only took a second of time to say. Added up across four years it was a memorable act of kindness. This way of living from a sense of good-will toward others only requires a simple and easy effort. In addition, he would answer a phone call by saying: "Hello . . ., what can I do for you?" This greeting also expresses a kind and caring attitude that improves our personal quality of life just by sending good intentions to others.

14

RELEASING LIMITS

Put no limits on anyone –including yourself. Start by releasing your self-limiting excuses. These excuses reflect the limits cast upon you from beliefs and traditions, customs and controls that have been blocking you from realizing your heart felt desires and dreams. Your dreams and desires are the unchanging thoughts and feelings that you've harbored deep inside you since early childhood. Choose one of those meaningful thoughts or feelings and think about how it would feel if you put it into daily practice.

Test that thought or feeling by taking a new step forward on your life-journey. Create a step that is meaningful to you, no matter your life history or present circumstances. Put your new step into motion. Does it bring feelings of joy and happiness into your being, your sense of self? Start with an easy step for this first experiment. Practice this step while it takes you past your comfortable, known and predictable ways of carrying out your daily activates and relationships. Hold true to your original thought or feeling and stay focused on your intentions, your dreams and desires. Practice this step forward until it feels comfortable, and continues to feel so good that you both happily and bravely take another step, and then another and another toward your highest visions for yourself. Trust yourself. Trust the guidance from your Inner-Child thoughts and feelings to keep you on track, and enjoying your dreams and desires along the way.

Take the leap to release limiting conditions and change directions in your life. Be open and willing to try-out new beginnings, new thoughts, new behaviors, new relationships, new habits –all by releasing limits on yourself and others. Release old ways of being, of thinking and believing back into the nothingness from which they all came.

Remember that you cannot fail as you let go of and release whatever is not fulfilling your sense of well-being. Remember that you always get more chances to keep moving forward on your life journey. Always stay true to yourself, and to what makes you feel good and happy. Support your thoughts and actions with kindness knowing that you are on the right track to fulfilling your dreams and desires.

Here are a couple of helpful tools to use along the way. They apply to every situation and are universal in nature. (1) With appreciation and gratitude accept all of the gifts that life brings along your way each day. (2) Remember to always treat yourself with kindness. Magical moments start there. The pleasure of being kind to yourself is enough to create a day of happiness for you to enjoy. Then, when you spread kindness to others the rewards multiply at ever-increasing frequency. The joy of expressing joy to others is a great bonus on any day, no matter what else is going on around you.

15

WRITING A NEW HISTORY

Many of us cling to our memories of past events, often repeating them verbally or in our thoughts. Especially prominent are the memories that charged us with strong emotional reactions. The memories may be anywhere in the range of scale from unspeakably terrible to speechless joy. If we're clinging to memories on the terrible side of the scale, those thoughts and beliefs are reflected in our daily lives in unpleasant ways. Whatever we think about is what shows up in our lives, either actually/literally or symbolically.

If you could take the unhappy memories and re-write them into believable action scenes, ones that make you feel happy throughout each day, would you do it? Give this exercise a try: Write down an unhappy memory that you often repeat in your mind. Then, start repeating in your mind the new happy version you are creating. Write out the new version of how you would have wanted the scene(s) to play out. Revise the new version as it develops and becomes more refined. Let the old version fade back into the nothingness from which it came, to the time before it happened. Be sure to feel your feel-good feelings about the new version. This exercise is an easy way of practicing forgiveness toward yourself and others for past actions. Go forward with your newly revised memory and make new memories along the same more desirable story line. Test the story line in your daily life. If this tool is helping to improve relationships, then we have a success story in action.

Now, how would you change the next memory, and the next memory after that? How would your life unfold so that it most closely matches your dreams and desires? Can you find a way through these revised memories, to release the emotions and forgive all who were involved? Each situation was the best performance that those involved could display at that time. No excuses. No blame. No judgment. It just was what it was. The memory doesn't need real-time correction. This rewriting exercise provides ideas about how to interact the next time we are in the middle of a similar situation. The better we handle each relationship interaction, the more knowledge we have to apply toward improved outcomes in future situations. We can always begin anew from where we are in this moment, by changing our thoughts and approach toward life events.

Remember that we can only be responsible
for our own thoughts and actions.

No one can change another person.

We all change our way of thinking
and our way of being
by our own design, by our own desires and decisions.

We each decide to be who we are
and how we live our life.

Can you create future memories of how your life will unfold before you? In your mind create your visions in vivid living color, with all of the sensations of sight, sound, touch, taste, and your feelings. How do your future memories feel to you? This is really important to feel the feel of your desired vision. How would you act? What would you wear? What would you say? See and act out the whole scene in your mind. Feel the feel of going through the motions to achieve the desired outcome. Then, practice your future way of being starting now, as if the future is already here. Keep practicing. What you practice will become your future. You will change.

This kind of creative visualization is similar to an activity practiced naturally by young children at play. Children practice role-modeling after observing their parents behavior. This is the way children grow up to sound, and act so much like their parents. See if you can rediscover this skill, making it a part of your daily life now and always. Enjoy yourself and have fun.

This is a personal journey, something that we each do for ourselves. We can only live our own personal life. Desired changes in our daily lives are realized through living by example. Mahatma Gandhi, a renowned historical non-violent civil/human rights activist in India, urged people to:

"Be the Change You Wish to See in the World."

Thirty or more years ago, I suddenly saw and heard a vision of a brutal hand-to-hand battle during deep meditation. It so frightened me that I quit practicing deep meditation. Not working past my fear and lacking trust in myself, I missed out on the benefits of meditation for about half a life-time. This was a hard lesson that finally taught me to let go of old thoughts, beliefs and ideas that are not serving my highest and best interest. We are not in this life to suffer, but to learn through our relationships, improve our role in them, and enjoy ourselves along the way.

16

HAPPINESS AND JOY ARE FREE OF CHARGE

May you easily pass through the burdens of daily life, by rediscovering the happiness and joy that is so often only enjoyed in early childhood. Young children express happiness and joy at every opportunity, even in the worst of living conditions. Rediscovering the child who is so in love with life, the child who still lives within each of us could bring fresh new meaning to your life. Easy to share, happiness is highly contagious.

Most people are so busy thinking about what they lack
that they don't take time to appreciate
what they already have.

For example: At the car repair shop earlier today I noticed a huge rainbow circling the sun. This one also had a radiating white light shining outward from the rainbow color circle. I wanted to share the beautiful sight. Starting with the office gal, she came out to take a look and then went after her sunglasses to get a better view through polarized lenses. Next, the owner came along curious about what we were doing oohing and ahhing while looking up into the sky. He disappeared and came back with his sunglasses. Then along came one of the mechanics with his sunglasses. There was a nice group of people appreciating a beautiful *gift of life*, as I drove away smiling at being able to share happiness and spread joy.

So many of the greatest joys in life
are free for all to enjoy.
These are the moments that cause us to pause
and take pleasure from the good feelings of
peace, contentment, relief, happiness, and joy.

Whenever you are doing what you enjoy, that feeling we have labeled as stress dissolves into the nothingness from which it came, taking muscle tension along with it. You are then left in a timeless state of happiness and joy, connected with your Inner Child.

Enjoy the events and activities, the sights and the sounds of your day. Experience each day in a way that makes you feel happy, brings joy and a sense of peace.

Practice, practice, practice.

17

BUILDING COMMUNITY

Genuine love comes from mutual respect.

With love from our heart-center, we can
create a great abundance of good-will.

Love brings us back across that line, when
we've lost the feeling of inner peace.

How do I rise up to handle this situation
with self love and self-respect?

How do I effortlessly extend kindness
and respect to myself and
to others?

We're in a moment in our society and globally when *authenticity* is key to human success.

Be true to yourself, to your innermost feelings about what makes you feel good. Use nothing but yourself to lean upon, to find your Inner-Child center of happiness and joy. Hold onto no other prop or a mask to hide behind. With genuine honesty, peel back the layers of self-defense and expose your true inner-self to yourself. You will discover a pure being of love. This is who you really are.

Ask yourself sincerely: "What do I need to know?" Quiet all thoughts of judgment and listen to your inner feelings, the ideas that pop into your mind, your reaction to what that you hear, see and feel through touch. How are your body and your mind reacting to the question?

If you don't like the feeling or what you are sensing, think the thoughts and feel the feelings for what you do desire. Keep your thoughts and feelings on the highest energy vibration possible, to be the happiest and healthiest possible. Remember that life flows most easily when we trust ourselves and follow our Inner-Child guidance.

Kindness and heart-felt love are keys to a life-path of experiencing happiness. Taking these values into our daily interactions and activities is the testing ground. Here is where we get practice experiences with feedback. We have to be ready for anything to come our way. How we react to daily events is part one. Part two is the quality of the feedback reaction. Did we like the response from life? Or, does our initial reaction need to be adjusted? Or, do our thoughts about our values need some adjustment? Sorting through and reviewing our thoughts is a life-long practice.

We use this tool for learning about our errors, undesirable past events and our interactions.

Following self-analysis, we can test the adjustments in our thoughts by looking for improvements in our relationship interactions. We cannot expect others to change their behavior and create a better relationship in our lives. We must each take responsibility to make the changes needed for improving relationships. We must each be the role model that influences others to make changes for improved relationships.

We are each that unique drop of water in the ocean of life. All of life, anything that we can imagine, and more, are the drops of water that constitute the ocean of life. Send thoughts of good-will to all of life and receive good-will in return. Unconditional acceptance of people and their varied ways of living, of thinking, (not tolerance, but acceptance) to let people be who they are as individuals builds community.

Just as you desire to live your life
according to your highest vision,
so does every other person on this planet
desire that same freedom for themselves.
We all deserve an equal chance at
living the life of our dreams.
Spread thoughts and actions of good-
will into all aspects of your life.
Life will respond in all sorts of kind ways.

18

APPRECIATION AND GRATITUDE

Look back on your life journey occasionally and notice the patterns in events. Notice how life actually does keep moving forward to better and easier living conditions, all according to our efforts made in that direction. Notice that we do progress to living a better life-style as we go along. This happens as we learn through the lessons, the training, the education, and the experiences of trial and error. Life does support our actions of good intentions and actions toward living a better life. Expressing appreciation and gratitude for our life experiences helps in bringing more of what we are grateful for. The law of physics that sends back in equal proportion whatever we give out is always a constant in our lives.

The journey of building a better life for ourselves starts early. As a young child we keep trying to walk, to eat independently, and eventually we succeed. This pattern of human nature continues throughout our lives. Whatever desires we send out with a sense of good-will do come back to us in some form that serves our needs.

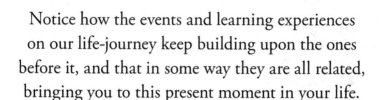

Notice how the events and learning experiences
on our life-journey keep building upon the ones
before it, and that in some way they are all related,
bringing you to this present moment in your life.

How often have your life events and experiences been
direct forms of your inner visions? Did you get what you
asked for exactly, or did it arrive in a different form, in a better
way than you had imagined? Your vision was good, but was
the result a much better vision for your life-path —one that
had not occurred to you? This is how life usually unfolds. We
usually get more than we ask for when our heart-felt feelings
and intentions are involved.

Some of the best things that we can do for ourselves
in this life are to enjoy our human abilities,
and to be grateful and appreciate the gifts-of-
abundance from a life lived with good intentions.

Start from where you are right now.
Take steps toward living the life of
your dreams and desires.

19

MAGICAL SURPRISES AND OUR INTENTIONS

One of the magical things about our life-journey is when our dreams and visions for our future are good, even great. And as we approach the culmination of a dream or desire, it presents in a much better way than we had imagined it to be. How many times has this happened throughout your life? Think back on events. Is it true that as time passed everything went along and then finished better than expected? So, why not make your visions be the best that they can be. Fill your visions with heart-felt love and compassion. Hold that picture in complete living-color detail in your mind. Feel the feel of your vision. Smell the smells. This helps bring it to life.

While bringing to life the vision of your desires,
be genuinely invested from your heart-center,
and this will speed the process for realizing your vision.

Invest your loving and caring self into doing whatever you can to make your vision be a part of your everyday life. This is the subject of a personal goal. Your action role is always personal. Live each day with your best intentions to be as kind as possible to yourself, stay true to yourself and keep going forward toward your highest visions for yourself.

This is the best approach and the most fun way of being a good role-model. Being genuinely open and honest is a *path of least resistance.* Clear your mind of any thoughts that are not serving your best interest. Focus upon all that is good and in the best interest for yourself and for others. As a young child this heart-centered genuinely honest behavior was all that we knew. Hark back to that time of pure honesty and check-in with the wisdom of your Inner-Child as you feel your feelings. Practice this tool when considering the moment-to-moment decisions that we all make throughout each day.

Visions come alive with our invested interests and efforts to achieve them. It is true that there is no "free lunch" in having the best of life's offerings. We always need to perform the steps that lead us toward the dreams and desires of our highest visions. Life supports us along the way.

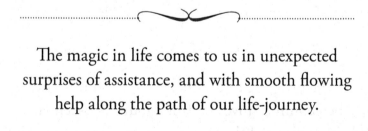

The magic in life comes to us in unexpected surprises of assistance, and with smooth flowing help along the path of our life-journey.

Acts of kindness are gifts from life. They boost our morale and our spirit of hope, helping us along our life-path. They are messages confirming that we are living in a way that is good for us, that is supporting our inner-growth in the direction of kindness and good-will toward ourselves and all of life. The happiness and the joy that we feel when recognizing the gifts from life throughout each day are also good indicators of being on a path for our highest good and well being.

A NOTABLE SECRET

The closer your inner vision to your
natural talents and interests,
the smoother your life path.

My vision story starts when I was in high school and beginning to learn how to downhill ski. I was hooked with passion after feeling the first sensation of sliding downhill across the soft snow. My first day on skis was a powder day, with about a foot of the fluffy stuff freshly falling by the end of the day. By day two or three of the lesson series, I understood that skiing technique progression for advancing to higher skill levels is very specific. I also observed that the better skiers fell less frequently. Falling without getting hurt is a learned skill. Getting up from a fall in snow is very tiring. Downhill skiing requires a high level of physical fitness. The more fit a skier, the easier it is to perform the movements necessary to turn the skis. All of these thoughts tied together added up for my wanting to learn how to ski at an advanced level as quickly as possible.

I started by visualizing myself perfectly performing the movements and body positions from the previous Saturday morning class. Eyes closed, looking inward, I brought my thoughts into picture form of seeing myself performing precisely the movements that were taught and physically practiced in that lesson. I engaged myself in this exercise every minute of the day that didn't require my attention on some present-moment activity. I visualized in bed each evening until falling asleep. At the next weekend lesson, I'd make good progress. I'd stay out on the slopes all day practicing the details of body geometry, taking maybe one short break, and always ending the day dehydrated and hungry. Eating an apple was the usual remedy. By the end of ten lessons I had gone from first time beginning skier to an advanced level skier (Austrian style.) That success just spurred me to reach my ultimate goal the following ski season, of being able to ski with anyone, anywhere, on any snow conditions. This did not include *getting air* (jumping.)

I do not know how I knew intuitively that seeing myself perfectly performing a movement would help me when physically trying to perform it. The general public in the Western world had not yet heard of visualization. It would be another fifteen years until Shakti Gawain published her popular book called *Creative Visualization*, and captured mainstream attention.

Visualization of our dreams and desires will take us to our heart-felt desires. Keeping our thoughts focused on what really matters most to us, the deep-seated feelings in our heart-center will unfold for us as we take steps toward those visions.

20

GROUP ACTIVITIES AND YOUR VISION

When involved in a group activity, our most personal feelings need to remain as our personal feelings. It is best to only share our feelings that are-based on thoughts and ideas relevant to the group topic or activity. Give cautious thought about the purpose of the group before introducing thoughts and ideas that are personal to you. Are they on topic and relevant to the mission statement goals?

Our personal vision may not be well received and insensitive feedback from others could be unsettling or upsetting to us. In the ripple-effect, there is the possibility of developing troublesome thoughts and that bring setbacks in our self-confidence. This is a path of downward-spiral thinking that could be avoided; as we monitor and carefully choose which of our most personal thoughts we share with others.

Also remember that as excited as we are about our highest visions, they morph in form and change as we move along our life-path. What appeals to us today may change tomorrow from learning new information, a thought we have or an event during the day. We tend to make uplifting spiral refinements, demonstrated as fine-tuning adjustments, as we move through our life-journey. Unforeseen experiences and opportunities take us along avenues that we hadn't thought of in our original visions. These are some of the reasons to consider, for keeping personal visions personal when working with a group. There are other ways to release our inner excitement about how well our life-path is unfolding before us. One way is to be our most authentic selves as often as possible. Support all of the good-quality components of the group with your words and actions. Suggest enhancement ideas that are easy to apply. Chances are good that they'll be well-received.

When performing daily activities and interacting from our heart-center in a genuine manner, the essence of who we really are is naturally expressed. Our thoughts are revealed through our words and/or our actions. There is usually no need to explain ourselves. Our words and gestures, our thoughts of kindness and love touch others, affecting their sense of being. Others see who we are at our heart-center. Their Inner-Child wheels instantly turn in the direction of being kind and loving. They want to feel more of the feeling they just received from an inspirational role-model. This happens without any effort on our part, or having to divulge our most personal feelings and thoughts by trying to explain ourselves. Sending out feelings of good-will toward others is enough.

Being non-judgmental and abstaining from gossip brings group participants together in a trusted relationship, and produces greatly reduced stress levels. This effect on a group is an astounding experience to be a part of. These were the two rules delivered to the new class entering a rehabilitation counseling graduate program. For the next year and a half we all lived each day without judging anyone or anything. There was an exception for the purpose of learning. Constructive criticism of our coursework was allowed. It takes constant practice (for weeks and months) to establish the habit of being nonjudgmental; and it is a practice well worth developing. As I continue to practice being non-judgmental, it makes life easier by softening the edges about my perspective on external activities and interactions.

The other rule we practiced was that no one was to say anything about anyone that they would not say directly to that person, as if the person was standing right there listening to what was being said. In addition, relating only first-hand experiences with another person was allowed. Also, any conversation about a person who is not part of the conversation is gossip. Even first-hand experiences are related from a personal perception of the interaction or event. Simple rules, yes? They are a challenge to follow until practiced for a while. The hardest part of embracing these rules was the reentry into mainstream society and workplaces. It was a wonderfully safe and innocent way to interact for a year and a half. In mainstream society, we can only do our part to be nonjudgmental and to avoid gossip. And, enjoy the occasional group who practices the same high standard of integrity.

21

SHARING YOUNG CHILDHOOD JOY

How can we find ourselves again, our child-like innocence of giving our love to others with reckless abandon in the face of the harshness in society? How can we stay true to ourselves, supporting our life-style, trying to reach our goals and dreams of an even better life? How can we recover the joy that brought smiles so easily when we were young?

We have tools at our disposal, tools that are stored within each of us. These natural tools can be called into service from our willingness to implement them. They are our natural-born talents and interests. Think back into your childhood, as far back as you can remember. List mentally, or record verbally, or in writing all of the things that brought you joy. Record every feeling of joy that you can recall up to this moment. Add to the list as your memory randomly brings recollections of past joy into your thoughts. These are your talents and interests. Build on what brings you joy! The first thing that joy brings is a smile. Smile with gratitude and appreciation for the joy of feeling joy. Life is a never ending series of gifts of everything imaginable. Receive gifts from life with joy. Share your natural gifts with joy.

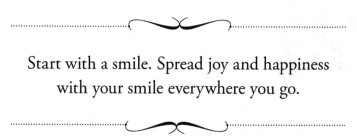

Start with a smile. Spread joy and happiness with your smile everywhere you go.

A smile costs nothing, but gives much. A heart-felt smile from you could be the best thing that happens to a person for that entire day. It may be the encouragement that was needed to recover from or to face a life-challenge that day. We have no idea the magnitude of good that an open-hearted smile from us can do for others. Share your smiles as often as possible. The gift to you is the good feeling that comes from uplifting others simply by sending heart-felt smiles.

22

STAYING TRUE TO YOURSELF IN A HARSH ENVIRONMENT

External demands forced upon how we live our lives can muffle and deaden our feelings of higher, more alive energy. Or, daily life activities can launch us forward into life-energizing experiences. All of our thoughts, every thought that we think is projected into our life experiences by what we say and do. Our words and actions tell the story of our life. The proof of how we live our lives is reflected in the quality of our good health and sense of well-being, our relationships, and the abundance of good offerings life provides for our enjoyment.

Common barriers that block our feelings of happiness and joy in daily life include: poor eating habits - addictions – disease – shame – guilt - stress – judgment – anger – unforgiveness – arguments – complaints – the need to always be right. All of these detriments to our happiness and joy come from fear-based thoughts. These life-energy depleting factors also depress and hide our creative abilities.

They fuel unhappy emotions that hold us back from enjoying a vibrant, creative life. Feeling unhappy, thinking unhappy thoughts, dwelling on the absence of what brings us joy, always yearning for whatever we don't have all attack and drain every part of our body, our sense of being, and diminish our daily activities. Today, stop all of that life-energy draining line of thinking. Instead, practice thinking about what brings feelings of happiness and uplifts our daily lives.

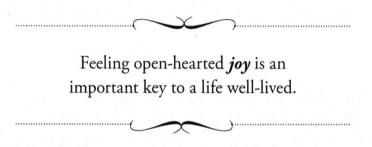

Feeling open-hearted *joy* is an
important key to a life well-lived.

And all along, society has been telling us that lots of money and living life in the fast-lane is our key to success. Instead, our life-supporting wealth comes from within each of us, from our intentions, from our thoughts and actions. Our wealth gauge is reflected back to us in the quality of our relationships, the happiness, joy, sense of peace, of safety, and well-being that we feel each day.

The more often we focus on staying true to our intrinsic/personal values, the stronger the external support comes from life-improving opportunities showing up in the right place at the right time. The big breath-taking surprises usually only occur once in a while. Magical moments that are equally important happen more frequently, as we pay closer attention to noticing them. Pay no attention to the distractions of a harsh environment. Pay close attention to the evidence of magical moments occurring on your behalf.

- Being true to your Inner-Child self in a harsh environment can be done.
- Finding peace and even joy in a harsh environment can be done.
- Holding true and trusting your feelings in a harsh environment can be done.

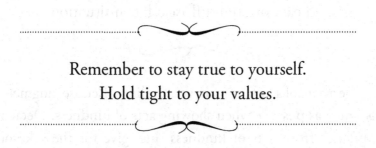

Remember to stay true to yourself.
Hold tight to your values.

The tools to survive a harsh environment involve being nonjudgmental as you interact with others. Send out thoughts of good-will toward others. There is tremendous inner-strength helping you hold your ground when sending genuine feelings of kindness toward others. Even when stern or strong actions to hold your position become necessary, act from a heart-centered intention. Feel and extend kindness toward others as you stand in your sense of truth.

Offering kindness earns gold stars for the one giving.

Kindness provides a win-win
platform for any situation.

Extending kindness can take people by surprise
and ease or even diffuse a harsh situation.

Be aware of any tension in your feelings. Release judgment as much as possible when showing acts of kindness. Detach your ego from acts of kindness. Just give for the sake of giving, to help make the situation softer and less harsh.

The summer heat in the American Southwest deserts creates an extremely harsh environment. Even that harshness can be mitigated in a naturally gentle way. I was just a kid somewhere around ten or eleven years old. I can still see myself sitting on a concrete slab, back against a concrete block wall. It was in the shade, but even in the shade the air temperature was in the mid one hundred teens, at least. It was oven-like hot outside everywhere. It is the kind of heat that feels like the bare skin on your arms is burning, like sticking them in the blasting heat of an oven ready to cook the evening meal. I don't recall why I was sitting there. My best guess is that I was in timeout for the latest rule infraction. It was a strict upbringing. Regardless, there I was and couldn't leave. It was hot and I was kind of thirsty, too. So, I made the best of the situation with nothing to do but just sit there.

I turned my thoughts toward feeling less hot and less thirsty, slowed down my breathing, and relaxed my muscles. That felt pretty good, so I took this slowing down process to the next level and focused on slowing my heart rate and blood circulation. All along I continued to imagine myself feeling cooler and less thirsty. It worked. The timeout was well-spent, and I have been practicing these techniques in a variety of situations ever since.

A decade later this process would be identified through medical research and labeled as Biofeedback. It continues to be a popular practice in the medical community, and the internet has good information about it.

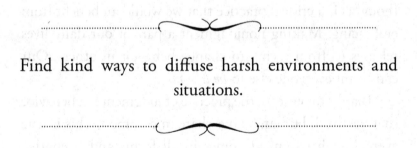

Find kind ways to diffuse harsh environments and situations.

23

PRACTICE NONJUDGMENT -FIRST WITH YOURSELF

It is a wonder of human nature that it is always easier to help others through difficulties in life than it is to work through our own difficulties. Releasing judgment from our thoughts is a critical practice that we would all benefit from embracing. Making nonjudgment a part of our daily lives releases us from trying to change behavior in others. Our egos want everyone else to *be like me.*

Thanks to our ego, the practice of judgment is a behavior that nearly all human beings share in common. This is true even though judgment comes in all forms and strengths, justified and unjustified. A brief exception is found in early childhood. There is no place in the world of wonder enjoyed by young children that includes judgment. It's a life-defeating habit that probably started when the first reprimand was directed toward us.

AN IMPORTANT SECRET

There are tools to keep judgment under control, and even eliminate it from our lives. Daily life becomes oh so much sweeter after banishing judgment from our lives.

Say you have loving feelings for another person and that person judges you with an off-hand judgmental comment. It leaves you stinging. It's now harder to keep the same love feelings flowing. Some trust in that person was lost after receiving the judgment comment. What about the times when you sling out judgment statements toward others? Do you ever wonder about how they're feeling about being judged? Even if you judge yourself as being justified for slinging judgments toward others, the receiving end person's feelings are stinging. And, does slinging judgments bring you joy and happiness, ever? Do you see the pattern? Judging others makes neither the sender nor the receiver happy. Being smug and self-righteous is not a replacement for being happy. What about the times when judgments are made in anger? These are the type of judgments that can highlight the evening news broadcast. Do you see the pattern?

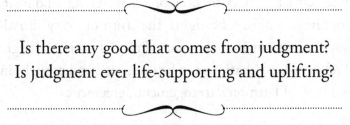

Is there any good that comes from judgment? Is judgment ever life-supporting and uplifting?

A certain form of judgment called constructive criticism or a critical review can be wonderfully helpful when offered in a respectful and caring way. It is typically given to help improve a product or behavior. In a family or intimate relationship situation, pose a gentle and loving suggestion for trying a different way of being; or, frame your constructive criticism as a question. This approach allows the receiver to decide about the personal validity of the idea offered for change. The suggestion may or may not resonate with the one who is receiving it. Discussion can follow. My typical unthinking reaction has evolved from 'no' to I'll think about it. Then, after some thought and visualization about the process and possible outcome, I'll give the suggestion a try. If it resonates with me, I'll adopt it and let the old way of doing whatever it was go back into the nothingness from which it came.

Blatant judgment is completely unnecessary, especially in friendly situations like this close relationships example. The results of judgment produce anger, blame, resentment, and so on. Instead of breaking down relationships with judgment, build them up with respectful communication. Seek understanding and discuss a common ground from all sides of a disagreement. Find resolution that brings feelings of good-will and an attitude of cooperation for all who are involved in the situation. This is easier to practice than it may appear. Give it a try. Also, keep practicing being kind instead of needing to always be right. The truth of every situation always comes out into the open. Proceed without judging. All relationship situations can be unraveled and brought into some level of harmony/arrangement/agreement.

The process of releasing judgment starts with ourselves.

If you have been judging yourself with painful harshness for many years, it is now the perfect time to change that behavior. Judging yourself is an emotionally harmful treatment that you have never deserved. It is time to give yourself a break and show kindness toward your gentle Inner-Child. It's that part of you who is filled with innocence and love and good-will and joy. Your Inner-Child is the best of who you are. Nurture the Inner-Child part of yourself with kindness instead of judgment. You deserve this kind treatment toward yourself.

Practice kindness toward yourself as much as possible, and as often as possible. You may be surprised at how many opportunities you discover each day to treat yourself with kindness. Always stop yourself mid-thought whenever any form of judgment arises. Change that judgment thought into a life-supporting thought. That is an act of kindness.

After some practice on yourself, start changing your judgment thoughts about family and social situations into life-supporting thoughts. Then share verbally with others your life-supporting messages. This is a challenging undertaking to eliminate judgment from the steady stream of thoughts, personal preference comments, and from conversations. Others around you may not be ready to take on this exercise. Make no rebuttal comments to judgment heard from others. Just work on yourself, on your part of releasing the practice of judgment, and enjoy the benefits of eliminating judgment from your life.

24

RECALL THE GOOD FEELING TIMES

Recall the times in your life when people made you feel good and happy, when you gave love and when you felt loved. Who were the people? What was their role in your life? What was the lasting effect they had on you? This recall activity helps us reconnect with our Inner-Child. It's our Inner-Child place of simple love and feelings of well-being where we find a sense of ease within our being.

Also recall the times when you did things for others with only the thought of doing for others. These may be harder to recall due to the altruistic giving nature of our actions. We may not consider our actions as being all that special. Even so, it's a good thing to be mindful that the energy of our thoughts and actions do radiate in an outward direction. In some way, either directly or indirectly, our thoughts and actions make an impression on everyone around us.

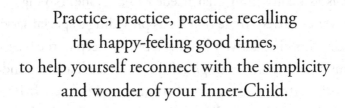

Practice, practice, practice recalling
the happy-feeling good times,
to help yourself reconnect with the simplicity
and wonder of your Inner-Child.

Keep making new memories for yourself and for others. Do this through acts of kindness coming from heart-centered thoughts of good-will. Keep a log, however brief, of the giving and of the receiving actions in your life going forward. It will help to reinforce this practice. New ways to serve others with kindness will come into your consciousness, now that you're more aware of interacting with others in this selfless way. This is an easy and powerful practice to bring more love into our lives and societies.

Remember to first serve your own needs, and then extend a helping service to others. Also remember to happily receive help from others. It is important to experience a good balance of giving and receiving. Balance in living fosters harmony in life.

It was some forty-five years or more and countless health setbacks later, when my failing mother stunned me. She suddenly reminded me of the summer I packed my Volkswagen bug (in the time before cars came with seatbelts) with six or seven grammar-school age synchronized swimmers after class. All summer long I drove them to their homes through the mid-day heat of the Mojave Desert (where Death Valley is located), to ensure their safe arrivals. It was just something that needed to be done. No big deal. It never occurred to me that I was providing a special service for the girls. The activity had been buried deep in the recesses of my memory files. I'm grateful for the feedback reminder, even thought it came around so many years later. **It is the little things of good-heart that really make the biggest differences in all of our lives. We never know who, when, or how we influence others with our actions**

Be of good-heart as often as possible. Spread joy.

25

THE ART OF LISTENING

The art of listening requires full sensory attention. This is the key to hearing the message. All other thoughts have to be quieted to listen and to hear the subtle and fleeting quiet voice of our Inner-Child thoughts and feelings. We so easily brush them aside with only a passing acknowledgment or no acknowledgement at all.

Catching the message at the first presentation, and then acting on it paves the easiest path for our lives. As we listen to the quiet voice inside us, as it comes to us in a fleeting thought, a feeling, follow the suggestion even if it seems silly or odd. Our life magically improves when we push past our barrier thoughts of knowing better. When we stretch our boundaries and follow the wise direction of our quiet, fleeting thought instead of allowing the loud exciting thoughts to prevail, our lives flow with much greater ease and harmony.

For instance: You are driving on a freeway and your Inner-Child wisdom says, "Take the surface street." Just do it without question. Later on while watching the local news, there would likely be a report of a major accident on the freeway just ahead of when and where you got off and onto a surface street. When following the fleeting thoughts of guidance from the wisdom of your Inner-Child, thoughts are enhanced as your focused listening skills improve.

Other messages come to us through our feelings. A common example is when not wanting to go out into the world and join in an activity, and feeling like just wanting to stay where you are. Or, there is a pulling desire to go somewhere else instead of staying where you are. Go in the direction that offers the most stability, like staying with family in lieu of an outing. I make this recommendation drawn from years of observation and listening to people relating that they were torn in deciding whether to stay or to go. Some went out of feeling an obligation and encountered life difficulties. Those who stayed had an uneventful experience of routine daily life. And there are stories of leaving that have saved lives. Just go with the feelings that lean toward peace and comfort.

Each subtle and fleeting quiet message from our deep inner wisdom will continue to resurface until we follow the guidance. Repeated messages become increasingly louder and stronger in demonstration throughout our relationships and life activities. This will continue until we finally have enough of suffering the pain from not following our own Inner-Child guidance. It will stop when we scrape the bottom of the barrel of life-struggle and change direction toward a more life-sustaining way of living.

We are constantly receiving inner and outer messages to help guide our lives. They are all meant to serve us for living the best quality of daily life. It is just that we are so busy thinking about how we know what we are doing, that we miss hearing/ sensing/feeling the incoming messages. We are usually running a stream of repetitive thoughts that are mostly non-productive. Common thoughts are judgmental and complaining, or worry and fear oriented. All of these examples are a waste of our time in this life. Dwelling on these themes brings us more of what we are fretting over, more of what we are not wanting. We get from life what we think about.

Always think about what you do want.

Turn every negative statement into a
positive statement of intention.

Listen to and follow the wisdom of your Inner-Child.

When not required to think about a work task, or some other activity of daily living, practice quieting your mind and listening. With thoughts quieted, start by being in a state of silence. Then, silently observe life activities as they are going on around you. Observe and listen without labeling or making comments to yourself. Just observe life from moment to moment, as if seeing it all for the first time. Look around, trying to catch all of the details of having a new experience.

This exercise can take a lot of practice to get good at it. Keep practicing. The payoff is tremendously fulfilling.

When completely focused on a task, all else around us is blocked out of our thoughts, even our other passing thoughts. We may remain vaguely aware of activity around us, but it isn't part of our focused attention. Our sense of time is suspended and forgotten when we are completely focused on any point of our consciousness. This is the condition needed to practice of the art of listening. This is the space where we hear the subtle and fleeting quiet voice of our Inner-Child thoughts and feelings.

The easiest way to focus in silence is to observe our breathing, the movement of air moving in and out of the passageways in our body. Just observe any passing thoughts as they drift across the movie screen of your mind. Pay no attention to them. As thoughts flow by, keep from stopping and dwelling on them. The thoughts of your mind will quiet down and take a break, as you more fully turn your attention toward listening to and feeling the wisdom of your Inner-Child.

Focused attention is also required
when listening to others speak.

Our thoughts can wait in the wings
of our consciousness.

Our quieted thoughts will be there waiting for us when
the person we are listening to has finished speaking.

For example: Focused attention is especially important when listening to a teacher. The only way to learn is to listen with our internal chatter quieted. Listening with a quiet mind is the only way to know what questions to ask for gaining clarity, to understand the information presented. During conversations, put self-centered and judgmental thoughts aside and simply listen to what others have to say. Hold aside your thoughts and comments until there is a pause when you can voice what is important to you. Or better yet, voice your reflection on what was said, to prompt further discussion, or to gain clarification.

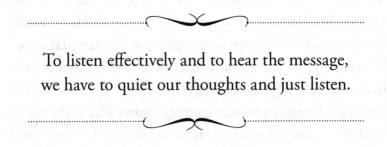

To listen effectively and to hear the message,
we have to quiet our thoughts and just listen.

26

Uncluttering Our Lives

To clear or even reduce the various types of clutter in our lives, to the extent that we lived as young children, would not be practical for our nearly global-wide material goods infatuation. In some way we all live with clutter in our lives. External physical clutter is the easiest to recognize and clear out. Internal physical clutter requires diet and exercise changes to shape up muscle tone, while clearing out excess fat; and, we're all familiar with that line of conversation.

Internal clutter is something that we may not have considered before now. Be it physical stuff, mental stuff, or emotional stuff, much of it is extraneous and superfluous. Clutter in any form clogs our life-path with obstacles. To unclutter our lives is to live more closely in alignment with the wisdom of our Inner-Child. It allows us to live more simply and free of unnecessary thoughts and actions. Uncluttering our lives leaves vacant space, creating an opening for physical, mental, and emotional stuff that is currently meaningful and important to our dreams and desires, as they lead us toward fulfilling our highest visions for our life.

External physical clutter trips us up as we are trying to move around, it hides things that we are searching for, and among other things it takes up space on the shelf for more meaningful stuff. The extra physical stuff in our lives deteriorates from lack of use. We forget that we even have the stuff, make unnecessary trips to the store to purchase more stuff to replace the stuff we already have, that will reappear some day while we're looking for something else amidst the clutter. Here is the drill: Completely organize the physical clutter by putting all like things together. Store stuff in places where it will be used, or the best place to access it for use. Give to shelters and charities all that is really not needed and will not be used any time soon –probably never. This is how to organize physical stuff quickly and easily. Then, always put things away in their designated storage place as soon as finished using them. Done.

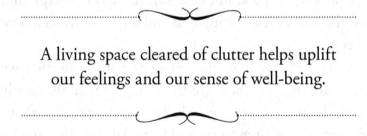

A living space cleared of clutter helps uplift
our feelings and our sense of well-being.

Filling our lives with the clutter of excessive activities and commitments is another area that needs organization. It is related to physical clutter by creating delays and detours in our daily schedules. Quite literally we run ourselves into a frazzled state of being. Then we get short-tempered and cranky, upsetting ourselves and everyone around us. We need time in our days for peaceful living. Take on only what is most important for supporting meaningful inner-values, instead of activities that merely feed a social image. Let go of activities and commitments that mostly serve to promote popularity and accolades. Even when our intentions are for the highest good for all involved, we have to choose between living a crazy hectic life or one that brings peace, joy and happiness to our sense of being. Choose activities that support the highest visions of life for ourselves, and that are uplifting for those who are close to us.

Remember to keep in mind that any improvements made to our internal physical clutter will bring benefits for better navigating daily activities. Just think about the possibilities. The healthier we are, the more life-energy we have for daily activities. We humans, like every other animal are not designed to live with aches and pains. They are not normal or healthy. Adopt a lifestyle that eliminates aches, pains, and dis-ease. Feeling good in every way, full of life-energy, and with the vitality felt in happiness and joy is our natural state of being.

Mental clutter is composed of the thoughts that we persistently repeat. These are the thoughts that are mostly nonproductive. Common clutter thoughts are about judgment, complaints, worry and fears. All of these examples are a waste of our time in this life. Dwelling on these themes just brings into our lives more of what we are not wanting. We get from life what we think about. Unclutter the unwanted thoughts from your mind by only thinking about what you do want. The unwanted thoughts will go back into the nothingness from which they came.

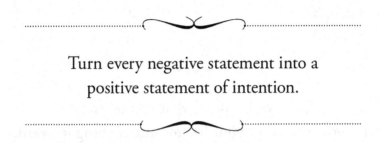

Turn every negative statement into a positive statement of intention.

Emotional clutter is the collection of all of the memories you are harboring that are labeled with resentment, blame, bitterness, jealousy, unforgiveness, anger, schemes to get even, schemes to punish, grievances, lists of injustices levied against you, and the fear-based list goes on. If this emotional clutter is not making you feel happy and bringing you joy, then it is time to unclutter your feelings. **It is a sure bet that the targets of your anger, bitterness, resentment, jealousy, unforgiveness and all of the rest of it, are not feeling the misery that you are imposing upon yourself by repeatedly thinking these harmful thoughts.**

Release your negative emotions through forgiveness. Forgive yourself for your role in the memory, and then forgive all others for their role in the life event. You don't have to re-enact any situations or reconnect with those involved. Just let it all go back into the nothingness from which it came. The important part is to let go of the emotions you have attached to the situation. You applied the emotions, and you can release them just as easily. Then move on and continue along your life-journey, freed from the self-imposed bondage of unwanted emotions. It helps to send thoughts of good-will to replace negative thoughts. Move forward thinking only the thoughts that take you in the direction of your dreams and desires.

Think only about what you do want
and how you want your life to unfold going forward.

Keep your thoughts and feelings
heart-centered as often as possible.

27

ALLOW EACH DAY TO FLOW FREELY

Stop pushing against whatever you don't agree with in your daily activities. Allow all of life to just "be" and to unfold in a natural way: This includes allowing yourself, others, situations, thoughts, ideas, decisions, and whatever else presents in your life to express in a natural/organic way. Allow every situation, encounter, interaction, activity to unfold without your personal leverage trying to resist it, or to control it.

Let it be (you name it), and let whatever is happening unfold without trying to control the action with your sense of right and wrong. Stay in your heart-centered feelings and observe without judgment. This is a worthy challenge to observe a situation from a neutral, nonjudgmental perspective, and to let it be and unfold in whatever form that has been put into motion. If anything, add kind-hearted support when needed to help the life event succeed in the best way possible. Practice this skill, and keep on practicing. Hold to your highest visions for yourself, for your daily interactions, and for the relationships in your life. Keep practicing.

When we manage control of
ourselves in a supportive way,
allowing life events to flow and unfold organically,
feelings of community cooperation
and good-will percolate
throughout the process.

A city girl in the office where I worked had never gone camping. So, I agreed to take her, her sister and a friend of theirs to the closest mountain campground for a weekend of outdoor living. Their car was our transportation, but at the close of the first evening I insisted that they give me the car keys to keep safely tucked away. They were all up far too early the next morning. After some pestering, I sleepily relinquished the car keys to them. In just a few short minutes they had locked the keys in the car, in the trunk. Finally, the commotion drove me out from the comfort of my sleeping bag. I fixed them the traditional camping breakfast of bacon, eggs, and pancakes. All the while they were trying everything they could possibly think of to get inside the trunk and retrieve the keys. They took a break and ate breakfast. As they returned to their mission, I washed up the dishes and tidied up the camp kitchen. With really nothing else to do, I sat on the picnic table and watched their activity. As a group of other campers was walking by I was struck by inspiration. I hailed to them, explained about the keys being locked in the trunk. Everyone squeezed together and lined up with both hands of our fingers along the underside of the trunk lid. There were enough hands to go the entire length of the edge. On the count of three everyone lifted up and the trunk lid opened with ease. Magic happens.

Allowing the morning to unfold without trying to control anything brought me a sense of peace. With the keys in hand, we drove off to a trail and did a little hiking. It was their first hike ever in a mountain forest. They all enjoyed their camping trip. Everything was new to them.

Love where you are in your life journey. Express appreciation and gratitude for all that you have in life and know that it all supports your way of living. Know that every day is better than the day before, as you continue to move forward in appreciation and gratitude for what you now have, and as you move in gratitude toward your highest vision of your life desires. To love and to be loved is usually romantically reference in most everyone's vision. There is so much more to love than romance. Regularly practice appreciation and gratitude from your heart-center. You'll notice that daily events flow ever more easily and are more often magical. This is a very powerful form of love.

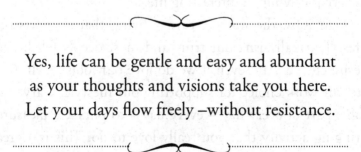

Yes, life can be gentle and easy and abundant
as your thoughts and visions take you there.
Let your days flow freely –without resistance.

28

PRACTICE AN ACTIVITY EACH DAY THAT MAKES YOU FEEL HAPPY

Do whatever you enjoy doing during some part of each day. Schedule an activity that makes you feel happy, makes you smile and that makes you feel at ease and feeling good inside. Choose an activity that brings you joy and a sense of peace. Schedule the activity right along with meals, body maintenance, and sleep. This special activity is an important part of your daily self-care. It serves as a reconnection with our Inner-Child. The activity may change depending upon the day of the week, or season of the year. It is good to have variety for living an interesting life.

Our jobs, the way we earn a living that supports our lifestyle usually isn't our truly and most deeply felt heart's desire choice. And even if we do love our job(s), well, they are our work choice for supporting our lifestyle. Carve out some part of every day – every day – to pursue a pleasure-bringing activity that you really love to do. This is a great emotional-pain releasing and dis-ease healing practice.

Pursuing pleasure-bringing activities can even restore wounds received from interactions on the day currently in progress.

We all have multiple activities that we love to do. Choose the one that feels the best to you in the present moment and enjoy yourself. Immerse yourself in the activity. Let the sense of time dissolve into the nothingness from which it came. Just focus on your pleasure activity and heal. The day will be there waiting for you when you return to it. Your Inner-Child will thank you for the play time by prompting you for more frequent and longer play time sessions.

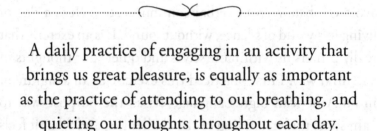

A daily practice of engaging in an activity that
brings us great pleasure, is equally as important
as the practice of attending to our breathing, and
quieting our thoughts throughout each day.

Check out the *Mind and Body Exercises* in the *Appendix*.

29

A DAY IN SILENCE

This is not the usual day of silence where we would typically avoid or abstain from verbal communication. It is a day of living in a world of silence, without sound. It is an exercise that really centers us within ourselves and quiets our thoughts in a natural way. I first practiced this exercise as an assignment in an American Sign Language class. The purpose was to gain some understanding of the challenges, and what it feels like to experience daily life being deaf. And, I learned more than expected from the assignment. It is an exercise that takes us within our being, where we are left with listening only to our inner-self. In the silence we can hear and sense the wisdom of our Inner-Child. Also, remember to feel the feelings that surface throughout the day. This is an exercise of self-exploration that is both powerful and comforting.

With good sound-deadening earplugs worn all day, there are some important things to keep in mind. Be extra careful crossing a street. You'll have to look around quite a lot to keep safe. Driving a vehicle also requires a lot more looking all around at traffic. If necessary to communicate in person, write your message and get a written response. Earplugs blocking external noise really enhance the inner-reference experience when in public places, especially when there is a lot of activity going on all around

An occasional day of practicing complete silence from external noise, and being in a place of inner silence is an interesting exercise. It gives us an opportunity to just observe, relax, rest, and look all around. We can more easily let thoughts pass through our consciousness, like a leaf floating past on a stream. Just feel the feel of being in silence.

When out in nature, my preference would be to skip the earplugs in trade for listening to the sounds of nature. If out in nature far enough from civilization, silence is common. Wind can be noisy, especially the sound made by air passing through the wings of a low-flying large bird. This is not the sound of wings flapping. There is no flapping noise, just the whoosh of air whistling through feathers. It is the only sound for some brief seconds in the otherwise complete silence of an early morning in nature.

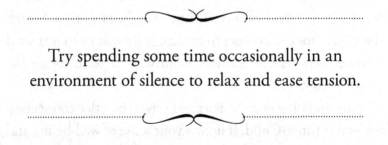

Try spending some time occasionally in an
environment of silence to relax and ease tension.

30

SENDING OUT SMILES AND GOOD-WILL

Our Inner-Child doesn't have a daily agenda. Our unleashed Inner-Child goes about each day with an open-heart, sending feelings of love out to all of life. You'll know when this is happening to you. You will feel a sense of peace and joy coming from your heart-center. Your stomach and other muscles will be relaxed as you feel at ease. You'll feel amazingly alive.

Try feeling a sense of open-hearted love on your next shopping excursion. Cruise through the store with the feeling of an open-heart sending out love feelings to everyone you see. Look at everyone in your line of sight as you go. Search their faces for eye contact to exchange a smile or to just send a smile their way. It really is a fun way to get through the shopping detail.

The shopping exercise is a great way to practice connecting with your Inner-Child. It uplifts your sense of well-being, and it also uplifts the feelings of others you encounter. We have no idea the magnitude of impact we make with the small gesture of giving a smile to another. Do know, that every smile you send out to another person makes a positive impact on their feelings. The reward is that you will automatically feel better for having sent out so much good-will into your surroundings. This is your Inner-Child having the best of times.

IMPORTANT REMINDER

Smiles are not gender or age specific
in either the giving or receiving.
Everyone benefits from a smile.

31

ROUTINES AND STABILITY

Routines, dependability, and predictability all point to stability. The Inner-Child in all of us craves stability. It helps us to feel safe. If a daily routine has been scarce through the course of your life, think of the times when you did feel safe, stable, and when life was routine, dependable and predictable. Recreate and build upon those memories so that they can be applied to your daily life now. This way you'll have a familiar place to turn to for comfort and relaxation. It is within this place of stability when the feeling that *all is well* rings true.

If you have no reference for a regular routine, design one for yourself. Keep it simple to start out with, because it will require adjustments along the way as you make life changes. Depending upon your thoughts and where they take you on your life-journey your daily routine will change.

Keeping to a simple daily routine takes the burden from trying to perform a busy itemized schedule. All a busy schedule does is frazzle our nerves from the pressure to perform. To start, design a routine of things that you would typically already do most days –some necessary things and some for fun. Just arrange the activities into an ordered fashion of when to do what each day –instead of doing things randomly, or skipping some days. For example: Brushing teeth is a good activity to include; making your bed each day upon rising; washing the dishes before going to bed each day, or at least putting them all in the dishwasher; going for a walk each day. These are just examples. You'll know what is best for your daily routine.

Difficult as it may be, try leaving everything out of your simple routine plan that can possibly be set aside. Make a list of all items put on the sideline. When the need or desire arises within you to attend to any of those items, they will be there waiting for you. Meanwhile, enjoy a more peaceful daily routine.

Just choose simple, easy things for a daily routine. Also, leave chunks of some unscheduled time to do nothing, or for being spontaneous to opportunities that suddenly appear. Follow the simple routine for a week or so and check-in occasionally with your Inner-Child. Feel your feelings and ask yourself, does this routine work for me? Try making some adjustments that better suit your needs and desires as the days go by. This is a personal journey. You are the best person and the most qualified to customize your life. The goal is to make your life easier and more peaceful.

32

OUR PHYSICAL HEALTH

Keeping ourselves physically healthy, to the highest degree possible, is important for the balance in sustaining a good quality of life. Being physically healthy is something that *everyone* can practice. It largely depends upon the food and exercise choices that we make each day. Even years of poor eating habits and lack of enough regular exercise can be turned around at any age. The more birthdays we've celebrated when not focused on maintaining a healthy body, the tougher the rebound to a physically younger body and higher, more youthful energy level. Even so, good physical health can be attained with a "can succeed" attitude and by following a health-oriented regimen.

A woman I knew was well into her seventies and about a hundred pounds overweight. She mostly sat and had trouble walking any distance, even inside her home. Stairs were nearly impossible to navigate. Within a year, she was back into wearing size 10 clothes. To rebound, she ate small portions of only nutritious foods needed for her body to be healthy;

and, she exercised her way back to more vibrant health. With renewed energy she could ride her horses again. Remember, this woman is well into her seventies. Another woman, who is in her eightieth year, has maintained her physical fitness through the years, keeping her weight in check by only eating what her body needs to stay healthy. Fruit has been her sugar source. She has lived a life of wellness, can still run and jump, and enjoys her lifelong favorite outdoor sports activities. A neighborhood couple are also hovering around their eightieth birthdays. They golf and play tennis multiple times every week during the three warmer seasons, and during the winter he downhill skis as many days possible each week. Similar "older" folks are increasingly more common in our American society, like the 92 year-old woman who gardens and drives her great-grandson to activities. She too can still run and jump, is slim and trim, looking good in her blue jeans.

If we are going to wake up each morning, we might as well make the best of our opportunity to enjoy the new day to its fullest potential.

Consistently eating a highly nutritious diet of proper portion sizes and walking or pedaling some miles each day, enough to break a sweat, are the minimum that is required to improve and maintain good physical health. It really doesn't take a lot of effort or time out of our day to practice a simple healthy lifestyle.

Just consider this: Instead of floundering in the eddy of health-crisis control, doctors could be morphing their practices into a whole new arena of aiding their patients to live the most vibrantly healthy life possible. Doctors could be enhancing wellness rather than constantly battling disease. This is a vision that could be realized in the very near future. If enough people in the developed nations really stayed with a habit of eating highly nutritious foods, along with practicing regular sweat-breaking exercise, this vision for most people to live through life without constant pain and dis-ease would be a success.

We all need to be mindful of what chemicals we are putting into our bodies. Only take in the ones that are life-supporting and that are sourced straight from nature to consumer.

The human population on this planet continues to grow. Living conditions are increasingly more crowded. Huge tracts of farmland are being turned into household communities every year. The United States imports increasingly more food from other countries each year, because our farmland now has a house and yard sitting on it. The United States is only one example among other countries around the globe with exploding populations. Changing our approach to the care and feeding of our physical bodies may have to be a priority for species survival.

This concept of eating healthy food choices and sweat-breaking exercise is worth consideration, especially for anyone who would like to feel more vibrant and alive throughout each day. Modern medicine cannot "fix" all of our maladies every time, especially when we aren't doing our part to help ourselves as much as possible. At some point, we each must take some personal responsibility for the quality of our health and well-being.

Living in a blur of pain is not our natural state of being. Constant pain and dis-ease makes us feel cranky, grumpy, resentful, bitter, and just plain mean, along with all sorts of associated self-defeating thoughts and feelings. The travesty is that most pain could be avoided by consistently eating a highly nutritious diet and practicing regular sweat-breaking exercise. Be certain to first consult with your primary care physician before starting any new health-improving regimen

Think back through the years and recall your early childhood days when feeling physical pain. Even when taking a tumble, the pain was gone in the few minutes of time spent crying about it. The pain forgotten, the adventure of life once again grabbed our attention, immersing us back into the joy of life. Let go of dwelling on thoughts of pain and suffering. Instead, think about life-supporting activities that will help relieve the pain. Embrace the thoughts and feelings of enjoying these activities with renewed agility, and put some bounce in your step. Your Inner-Child will thank you with feelings of happiness and joy.

As a toddler I fell and split my lip open on the fireplace hearth. The scar from a couple of stitches is the proof. I don't have a conscious memory of the incident. The earliest serious pain that I can clearly recall was at four to five years old, after falling off a little donkey. During the scuffle of rescuing me the donkey accidently stepped on my back. That hurt. The fall was nothing in comparison. So, I cried for a while, sitting on my grandmother's lap in the kitchen. As soon as the tears stopped, I was ready to head back out and finish the riding lesson. The pain was mostly gone and life was moving on. *Our bodies are self-healing machines.* The important message from this story is to let go of pain from past experiences as soon as possible and move forward, embracing the joys and wonders of life moving forward. This is something that we never out-grow and can practice throughout our lives. No matter how serious we become in life, there is always room for embracing the joys and the wonder of life. And with that, there is little room for feeling pain.

The better we feel physically,
the better our mind functions for decision making,
and without the mask of pain, the
better we can feel our feelings.

33

TRUSTING OUR INNER-WISDOM

Feeling the need to control our lives, other people's lives, and daily events is centered in fear –fear for our safety. Control is the armor we use to keep ourselves feeling safe from harm. If we are offensive, there is little room for being defensive; and ironically, that is our defense for feeling safe from harm. Emotional harm and physical harm are the most vulnerable areas of our self-defense. We typically spend our time and energy defending what we don't want in life rather than focusing on what we do want in life.

What if we focused on the aspects of daily living that help us feel safe and secure? What if we thought about actions that would bring us daily success in our activities, instead of worrying about what could go wrong? What if we trusted ourselves to make decisions each day that enhanced our safety? Trusting our Inner-Child wisdom brings peace to our lives, and a sense of inner-strength. Fears fade into the nothingness from which they came. Feel the feelings coming from within our heart-center, stomach, gut and trust them.

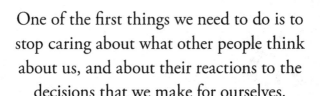

One of the first things we need to do is to stop caring about what other people think about us, and about their reactions to the decisions that we make for ourselves.

Live a life that is true to your inner/intrinsic values and you'll always be doing and saying the right thing at the right time.

It matters not at all what other people think of your life-decisions. If others have your best interest at heart, they will support your decisions. Those who really have your best interest at heart may express their concern for you, because it is something that they would avoid, but will still support you no matter your choices. Your ideas may not always resonate with others, even those closest to you. Know that staying true to your feelings and Inner-Child wisdom will be among your best-choice decisions for supporting your dreams and desires.

We all have the right to think freely and to live our lives according to our inner-guidance. No one can take that away from us. No permission is required for us to act upon what feels good and supports our sense of well-being. Staying true to the guidance from our Inner-Child keeps us true to our authentic self. This connection keeps us on track for expressing our inner/intrinsic values. This is a fail-proof, super safe and secure guidance system that we are born with. It's that part of us who feels from our heart-center what is the best next step to take on our life-path. Our life-path can always be adjusted to accommodate changes in our dreams, desires, and visions as we become more finely tuned into what really is important for our sense of well-being.

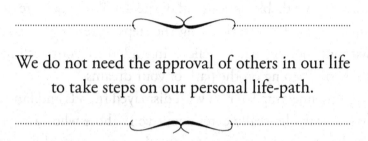

We do not need the approval of others in our life
to take steps on our personal life-path.

It does not matter what others think of our life-path decisions. We are the ones living our lives, not anyone else. Most "friends" and family, especially family members telling us how to live our lives, have their self-interests at heart and not our best interest in mind. The people who are close to us, who are trying to control our life-path really just want us to be a reflection of them. Their goal is to maintain their comfort and security, as they live in their world of self-imposed, fear-based boundaries. These are the nay-sayers trying to talk us out of our decisions and prevent us from following our heart's-desires. Do not fall into the trap of caring about what anyone thinks of our free-will decisions, as we move toward living the life of our dreams. As quickly and as gracefully as possible, get out of situations that feel uncomfortable. Seek the company of those who are supportive and who are interested in learning about different ways of doing and being in this adventure of life.

Leaving our friends and family behind (even if only temporarily) to follow our dreams is a radical step to take. It is an individual free-will choice that we make. Weigh your options. Weigh out all of the factors, and the strength of your desires and intentions, and the importance of your dreams. Make your decisions after examining all of the pros and cons, the workable options, all of the details of your dreams and desires. Then start taking the steps to reach your goal, without looking back. Believe in and trust your feelings. Keep on keeping on the path of your dreams.

Reconnecting later on with dismayed friends and family will reveal who really cares about you. Those who care will be the ones welcoming you, and who are interested in your journey and where it has taken you. Others will warm up to you as soon as they see that you are only an improved version of your old self.

In my twenties, I drove solo along the then unpaved, full of mud, curves and potholes highway through British Columbia and the Yukon to Alaska, with the intention of staying. My family was concerned for me, but said nothing to discourage my journey. When I returned some months later, my grandfather said, "I see you made it back." For the adventure that I was seeking, it was not the place for a young woman alone in rural Alaska. Had I gone down the road of stability, and stayed with my dental assisting job in Anchorage, I'd have probably fared better and stayed much longer. Following my Inner-Child wisdom when feeling in danger, I had made the quickest and most graceful exits possible, managing to return unscathed from (or not go when invited to) dangerous places. Making a connection with me, my grandfather followed with, "Let me tell you about when I was there in 1922, in the Merchant Marines." That was surprising news to me. I was fascinated to hear his stories, but he down-played them into unfinished mumbles, not wanting to out-shine my latest adventure. Mostly, he wanted to hear my stories of Alaska. That is a sure sign that a person cares about you.

Follow a life-path toward fulfilling
your inner dreams and desires.

Live your life without caring what
other people think about you.

We cannot please all of the people all of the time –ever.

Judgment fails to acknowledge or allow
expressions of opposing ideas.

Those who care about you are always there for you.

Some closing thoughts on trusting the wisdom of our Inner-Child.

- Why not make the best of your life, in the best ways that you are able to take action, no matter the circumstances?
- Go forward in life by following your heart-centered guidance.
- Be nonjudgemental. Go forward in life finding ways to understand, respect, and honor the opinions of other people.
- Do your best to understand the underlying reasons for actions taken by other people.
- Always be genuinely kind to yourself and to everyone along your path.
- Remember to smile as often as possible. Smiling at yourself in the mirror while honoring all the goodness of who you really are is great fun.

This about covers the basics of everything you'll need along the way of your life-journey.

34

FOCUS ON ALL THAT IS GOOD IN YOUR LIFE

Focus on all of the things in your life that are good, that support your sense of well-being, that make you feel safe. Think about even the most simple things that you appreciate and are grateful for having in your daily life: your shelter, food, clothing, family, friends, neighbors, all of the good and pleasant memories. Focus upon all of this throughout each day, just as a child delights in the things of life that bring joy to the moment. Express gratitude for the great abundance in your life. Let all else go by the wayside.

Pay no attention to unpleasant memories. Instead, keep repeating only the impressions of goodness from your memories; and your present moment good thoughts will bring improved future experiences. Your life will be easier, more pleasant, and your sense of feeling safe will increase. Even if the external world is in turmoil, you will still feel good and safe inside yourself. Your thoughts have created this haven of goodness in your life. Continue to create ever-new thoughts of the ideal life you are living. Feel the feel as you think the thoughts, and act them out as you go through each day. It is a lot like the way children pretend-play adult roles. Now you are older, and this is a way to practice living the life of your dreams in an easy and sensible way. Adopt what works for you as a regular way of living and keep trying new ideas that interest you.

Give your mind a break from thinking as often as possible. Observe each moment of the world in action around you just as a young child watches with awe and wonder. View as if experiencing life for the first time seeing, hearing, and feeling with your senses. When distracting thoughts disrupt the practice of your *first-time viewing experience*, use this tool:

> An easy way to quiet the mind and silence the chatter from thoughts is by observing your breath. Follow the inhale and exhale, by feeling the air entering the nostrils, passing through the nostrils, down the throat and into the lungs. Then briefly pause that breath before gently letting it out, following the exhale passage through the throat and out the nostrils. Just breathe naturally while observing your breath. And as you practice this exercise of observing your breath, just observe the activity of life around you without labeling or commenting to yourself. Observe as if seeing the activities around you for the first time, and continue to observe your breathing.

With each breath, also notice how your chest expands and relaxes. As thoughts try to distract you, discipline yourself to stay focused on your inhale and exhale, and just observe the action of the *breathe of life*. Practice this exercise for observing the breath as often as possible throughout your days. Enjoy the peacefulness within your being that this time of silence brings. This is the natural way of being for young children. They explore and feel the world with their senses, as they observe it without the chatter of verbal language. Judgment is unknown to young children. They view the world each day with a sense of wonder and curiosity. Try it for yourself –as often as possible.

Remember to make decisions by
checking in with the wisdom
of your Inner-Child in your heart-centered feelings,
and always treat yourself with kindness.

Adopting this frame of mind is worth practicing
for anyone who dreams of and desires the
experience of an improved quality of life.

When pausing to observe life in action,
we experience the many good things
that come our way each day.

Someday you may say "It's all good."
from an inner knowingness.

35

BEING YOUR OWN BEST FRIEND FOR LIFE

Throughout your life, who has always been there for you, no matter what? The people who have never failed you, but have always been at the right place at the right time, doing and saying exactly the right thing to help you feel good in that moment? Name them all. Who are they? Think of everyone who comes to mind. Recall the people who have passed through the ebb and flow of your life events. We are talking consistency here. Who always hit the mark, no matter what? Take some time to think through your life. Pause and recall interactions with the most special people who have helped you in wonderful ways along your life-journey. No one has been that consistently perfect you say? Not even yourself? There are times when even you have let yourself down? Amazing as that may seem, how could that be true? If our thoughts continue along this line of thinking, painful thoughts come creeping in, roaring in, and confusion blurs any joy. It's time to return to the original question: Who has always been there for you, no matter what? It is you. Even when supported and prompted by others helping to uplift you. You were the one who took action steps forward. You have always been there to pick yourself up and go again. Let's cultivate your relationship with yourself.

Number one, it is so very important to always be kind to yourself. No matter what, be kind to yourself. Treat yourself with respectful kindness. Care about yourself in a loving way. Nurture your Inner-Child of heart-felt feelings. You deserve this self-love. Always support your actions in a caring manner, even when you have made poor decisions. All errors can be corrected. Be your own cheerleader for creating a better life for yourself.

Forgiving yourself and forgiving past situations, interactions, your actions and the actions of others can improve every area of your daily life. Genuine forgiveness is life-changing. Forgiveness improves daily life in everything from relationships, creativity, finances, all health problems, and whatever else comes to mind. Forgive all that is of human nature. Release your emotional investment in the unhappy memories. Whenever familiar situations present again along your path, re-think your involvement in repeated interactions. Take nothing personally and be true to yourself. Remember that we all do our best in any given moment, with what we have to give in that moment. Avoid whatever you choose to avoid. Try again, whenever you want to reconcile a relationship. Just start anew. What has gone before has passed back into the nothingness from which it came. You are in the here and now moment. And, you'll not know how the action will unfold until you take steps in that direction.

Be open to making adjustments in a renewed relationship. What had gone before wasn't working. One cannot expect to repeat the same behavior and get different results. Albert Einstein labeled that approach as being insanity.

Relationships are necessary for living a life fulfilled. Living isolated as if on a remote island or deep inside a cave is a tough way to plow through life. It is so much easier to benefit from the gifts of sharing through trustworthy relationships. Listen to and acknowledge the thoughts and ideas of others. Give the ones that interest you a test-run in your daily activities. Adopt what ideas work for you and discard what doesn't. As you build the life of your dreams, keep trying new ideas to weave into and through your life. Relationships are made possible by sharing from the substance of ourselves and receiving offerings from others. Relationships do not survive by weighing in the direction of one opinion or another. Lasting relationships require a respectful balance of blended personal preferences. Express appreciation and gratitude often –for everyone and everything in your life.

There are some other human behaviors that are important to relationships, including the one with ourselves:

Complaining. Stop complaining. Stop immediately and never complain again –about anything. What we complain about is reinforced by the attention we give to the subject, just by complaining about it. More of the same subject-of-complaint will keep coming into our lives as we keep complaining about it.

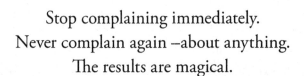

Stop complaining immediately.
Never complain again –about anything.
The results are magical.

Appreciate and Be Grateful for as many things as you are aware of during each day. Just say thank you for even the smallest and most seemingly insignificant things and experiences. A few of my daily favorites are a weather-proof place to call home, a constant flow of electricity and indoor plumbing, with hot and cold running water. These are huge gifts-of-life. I also give a lot of thanks each day for my abilities; the ones routinely applied to execute my activity choices for daily living. These are huge gifts-of-life. Expressing thanks for what you have brings more of those good things into your life. Remember to thank people you encounter for any actions of kindness.

Thank yourself for every reason you have during each day, to be grateful for your thoughts and actions. Appreciate your contribution to your quality of life.

Inner Strength. Appreciate your sense of determination to keep on keeping on through your life, no matter what. Practice life-supporting habits and activities to maintain your strength.

Be out in Nature. Spend some of each day (air quality permitting) enjoying the feel, sights, and sounds of nature. The natural environment is life-supporting and uplifting to our sense of well-being. The Spring and Autumn months have the longest sunrises and sunsets. So beautiful.

<u>Judge not</u>. If you knew better from a deep inner sense of knowingness, you would do better. Take note of corrections that you'd make when you get another chance at a similar situation and let this situation go. Move on through your day focusing your attention and thoughts on this moment and then into the next present moment.

Add additional line-items to this sample list that are meaningful to you.

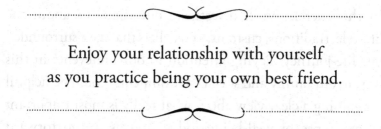

Enjoy your relationship with yourself
as you practice being your own best friend.

36

PLANNING YOUR LIFE-PATH

In this exercise we'll investigate our thoughts about the lifestyle, traditions, customs, and beliefs that have surrounded our life-journey. Paying attention to our life events in this way, to our family and social environments, could be helpful for gaining a clear view about what really is most important to our sense of well-being today, and as we go forward through our life-journey.

Create a list of the major influences (such as lifestyle, traditions, customs, and so on) that have influenced your life-path as they occurred throughout your life. Then, add your thoughts and observations to each category. This will provide a roadmap of the beliefs and feelings that are the strongest in your memory, and of your feelings about where you stand with them.

Next, reflect on each of the thoughts and observations, writing your reactions under each thought. This exercise is creating a hierarchy outline form. It is for your use only while exploring ever deeper into your feelings about the structure of your life-journey, up until today. Finally, read through each category and feel the feel of your reactions, to discover an even greater sense of clarity for understanding your true beliefs.

Start another list by logging these final reactions to the exercise. This one describes how you are feeling in this moment about the complex nature of each category. Revisit your work another day. Write yet another list of your reactions to each category. Repeat this activity a few more times and then compare your final reactions from the different days. Where are you seeing patterns in your thoughts? What do you think of the patterns? How do you feel like reacting to the categories of your life-journey, moving forward?

This is a nice self-inventory exercise. It fosters exploration of self-discovery in a gentle way, to better understand where your thoughts, ideas and feelings are vibrating today. There is no need to cling to past behaviors and activities if your ceart-Centered Inner-Child is pulling you in some other direction. Release feelings of obligation, guilt, and any shame that have been cast upon you by others. Those messages were intended to restrict you, holding you bound in a certain environment. Really scrutinize your thoughts and feelings about family customs and traditions. And then really scrutinize your heart-centered desires for living your life. It isn't an easy choice to make. It takes great courage to step outside family boundaries. Find the most gentle ways possible to live in the direction of your heart-felt dreams and desires; the ones that incorporate your interests and natural talents.

Always honor your life history. It has brought you to this moment, as you take steps in fresh new directions.

Epilogue

Love as a child gives and receives love.
Love unconditionally,
that is:
Love with non-judgment.
Love with acceptance.
Love with joy in your heart.
When it comes to pure love, we are *all* alike.

First forgive yourself.
Forgive yourself completely.
Honor your heart-felt feelings.
And, always treat yourself with kindness, no matter what.
You do not deserve punishment,
reprimands, or unkind remarks.
Strike all self-harm from any thoughts toward yourself.
And, always treat yourself with kindness, no matter what.
Be gentle with yourself in all ways.
Keep practicing.
Kindly and gently forgive and make peace with yourself
when not meeting your own standards of behavior.
Keep practicing kindness toward yourself in every way.
You are worth loving, of being loved.
First learn to love yourself just as you are in every moment.

Love from deep in your heart feelings
and fly high in the joy of loving and of being loved.

Sit in silence and feel the feel of heart-felt love.

Peace on earth and good-will to all.

APPENDIX

MIND AND BODY EXERCISES

Making the constant moment-by-moment decisions of choosing happiness outcomes for greater joy could stand an occasional break –by giving yourself a vacation from thinking. Offered here are easy and effective mind and body relaxation exercises. The exercises are also scattered throughout the book. The idea was that as the reader happens upon an exercise, it might feel like the thing to do, instead of continuing to read –to take a break from thinking and focus on breathing and body movements.

THREE BREATH EXERCISES

Breath Exercise 1 Mindful Breath of Life

As often as possible throughout each day pause and notice how you feel –in your gut, in your heart, in your head, in your muscles. Just observe.

Next, breathe in as you say to yourself one (1) to four (4) words of life values that are meaningful for you. Use words that bring a sense of love, joy, and happiness that uplift you.

Pause your breath, and then fully exhale saying to yourself words of release and relief that are meaningful to you. These are words that release tension and bring peace, good feelings and joy.

Notice how you feel. Then, return to your activity of daily living.

Over time, try out different words
till hitting upon words
that really move your inner feelings
from tension to feeling good
by the end of the exhale.

Go for words that are very personal to you.

Some word examples are: Love, Healing, Peace,
Joy, Release, Allow, Faith, Receive, Giving,
Bliss, Harmony, Trust, Patience, Patient, Kind,
Safe, Protected, Agree, Support, Courage.

— This exercise helps with pain relief for both physical and emotional distress.

— Breathe in Peace, Love, Harmony, Balance, Perfect Health.

— Breathe out Release, Stress, Anger, Resentment, Blame, Judgment, Fear.

— And, breathe out Love, Kindness, Community.

– Pause before the next inhalation and notice the level of muscle relaxation.
– Take another mindful breath and release even more tension.

This exercise is safe to practice while driving and riding vehicles. Years ago it helped keep my mind focused and energy level elevated, while motorcycle touring hour after hour along straight stretches of highway on those six and seven to eight hundred mile days.

Breath Exercise 2 Attend to your breathing.

Simply observing your breathing can be done anywhere at any time, 'round the clock. A perfect time to practice this exercise is while waiting -for anything. Stand, sit or lie down with legs and ankles uncrossed. Relax your tense muscles one by one. Quiet your thoughts, be still and attend to your breath moving in and out. It will naturally slow down as you relax. When thoughts enter your mind screen, allow them to flow through without stopping them. Just observe the passing motion picture as it pops up. If important, the thoughts will be there for you when finished with this exercise. Stay still in this relaxed state attending to your inhalations and exhalations for as long as possible. It is restful and rejuvenating for your energy and sense of well-being. This exercise also allows one to observe the external world in action like a silent movie passing by.

There is limitless variety in this adventure we call life.

Enjoy each day and the wonder of the
surprises that come your way.

Give yourself moments
of restful breaks whenever possible.

<u>Breath Exercise 3 Deeper relaxation.</u>

No matter who you are, your age, young or old, your
formal education does not apply, nor your place in society,
your talents, abilities or disabilities. Everyone can practice
and benefit from this exercise.

Allow all thoughts that come to mind just pass right on
through without pausing them. Be still, be relaxed. Relax
all of your muscles until feeling completely relaxed. Check
yourself from head to toe and out to the fingertips. Release
any tension. Be still without movement. If feeling the urge
to move, resist moving and relax any tense muscles. Attend
to your breathing, observing each inhale and exhale. Just
observe your breathing, the rhythm of your breath, the
expansion and relaxing of the diaphragm as air enters and
exits your lungs, pushed in and out with your diaphragm

below. Can you feel the gentleness, the softness in your heart-center now? –the calm sense of peace and relaxation? Keep observing your breath, each inhale and exhale. Check for any muscle tension and relax until no muscles are felt, just total relaxation –in stillness. Observe your breathing –each inhale and exhale. The tip of your tongue may naturally find a comfortable resting place just behind your upper front teeth. And your inner vision may tend to focus on the area of your forehead between and just above your eyebrows. Relax all muscles. Keep observing your breathing for as long as you feel comfortable. Notice the air as it moves on the inhale against the back of the throat, just under the nasal passage. This is a good focus area for an uplifting feeling on the inhale. It is helpful to practice this exercise a couple of times each day for as long as possible. It is great natural medicine for improving one's quality of life.

Giving yourself some time each day in silent relaxation enhances that comforting sense of well-being.

Practice this exercise while sitting in a recliner. Reclining in a hammock would also be excellent, especially if outdoors in a place where the temperature is comfortable. Hammocks also serve as comfortable beds, especially the handmade hammocks from the Yucatan Peninsula in Mexico. These are designed to recline in by stretching side-to-side instead of lying end-to-end.

FIVE TRIED AND TRUE
ENERGY-BOOSTING EXERCISES

These are easy muscle strengthening
routines to support improved posture,
and allow better energy flow through your body,
to feel happier and more alive/vibrant.

Remember to be gentle with yourself, and enjoy
the feel of muscles, tendons, and ligaments
moving to release pent up stress.

*STOP IMMEDIATELY at the first sign
of pain.* That is your current limit.
Keep practicing each day, even twice a
day, moving smoothly and gently.

1. <u>CHAIR EDGE REVERSE PUSHUPS</u> –for triceps, abdominals, and back muscles.

This is a great exercise for strengthening the back muscles. It helps alleviate the slouched posture that results from excessive chair-time in a sitting position.

- Sit on the front edge of a straight chair, a table chair without arms.

- Place hands at the corners of the front edge, next to your legs.

- Extend your feet out in front as far as they will reach while keeping them flat on the floor.

- Scoot off the edge of the chair seat, supported by your arms.

- Check your position to be certain that your lower legs are straight up and down. If not, you may have to scoot your feet out a little more.

- Lower your body down a little and then push up with your arms.

Start with as many repetitions that are comfortable to do. Gradually increase the number each day as your muscles strengthen.

As this exercise promotes good posture, it also helps tighten the triceps, that flabby flap under the upper arms. So many back and neck aches are a result of poor posture, commonly caused by our sedentary life-style of sitting for so many hours each day. Life was different in so many ways back when we still plowed the fields by hand and scrubbed clothes on a washboard. The tradeoff is giving up that exercise experienced through activities of daily living for our modern comforts and technology. Physical exercise now has to be scheduled into daily activities.

FIGURE 1 –CHAIR EDGE REVERSE PUSHUPS

Bonus Tip: Here's a way to reinforce this last exercise when sitting. Stretch the base of your spine toward the earth, and at the same time stretch the top of your spine toward the sky. Sit in this position as much as possible. The side effects are that this exercise also causes the abdomen to pull in tight and the shoulders to pull back. And sometimes, gentle popping will occur as the muscles release stuck energy. Also practice this technique while standing and walking. It helps with feeling good anywhere, at anytime.

2. SIT-UPS
KNEES BENT, FEET FLAT ON THE FLOOR.

Strive for a goal of doing at least 50 sit-ups per day –or as many more that feel good to you.

This is also an excellent exercise for supporting good posture.

3. STRETCH & BALANCE

This is a very helpful exercise for promoting balance when walking and moving about.

- To start, stand with feet about six-inches apart.

- Bring your arms together, stretched out in front, palms down.

- Keeping your eyes on the backs of your hands, rotate your upper body to the left.

- Keeping legs straight, with knees relaxed, and bend forward at the waist.

- As you bend, keeping arms straight, raise the left hand straight up, keeping your eyes on the back of that hand, looking up, palm facing toward the sky.

- At the same time the left hand goes up, lower your right hand toward the floor, with the palm facing down toward the earth.

Hold this position for a count of 5-10.

- Return to the starting position by slowly raising your upper body and bringing your hands back to the starting position, with your arms stretched out in front of you.

- Rotate your upper body to the right and repeat the steps.

Perform 3 times on each side.

At the end, relax with arms lowered naturally at your side.

FIGURE 2 STRETCH AND BALANCE

4. <u>ROTATE SHOULDERS IN UNISON, FRONT TO BACK</u>

ALWAYS MOVE SLOWLY AND GENTLY –RELAXING

Perform this exercise with hands relaxed in front at chest height, or with arms relaxed at your sides –whatever is most comfortable.

Stay as relaxed as possible, and make the rotating movements slowly and smoothly.

5 - 10 Rotations front to back.

FIGURE 3 ROTATE SHOULDERS

5. EYE MUSCLE ROUTINE

This exercise helps with eye movement strength and elasticity needed for vision. This routine only takes a few minutes and can be performed almost anywhere. Remove glasses, if possible. ---Keep your head still, facing straight away. Only the eyes move.

-Hold both eyes wide open throughout this exercise.

-Make each eye movement slowly. Slow movement is the eye muscle strength training.

-Slowly look straight up and pause for a second, holding eyes wide open.

-Slowly roll your eyes to the far left and pause for a second, holding eyes wide open.

-Slowly roll your eyes straight down and pause for a second, holding eyes wide open.

-Slowly roll your eyes to the far right and pause for a second, holding eyes wide open.

Repeat the counter-clockwise circuit 5 - 10 times. Change direction and go around in a clockwise direction another 5 - 10 times.

- To finish, close your eyes and gently place the palms of your hands over them. Turn your vision/focus inward, switching your thoughts to mute, and hold for a slow count of 30, or longer for greater stress relief.

ALTERNATIVE EYE EXERCISE VARIATION

Perform these eye exercise variations at alternate exercise sessions. This series is also very effective for helping eye movement strength and elasticity needed for vision.

- Keep your head still, facing straight away. Only the eyes move.

- Hold both eyes wide open throughout this exercise.

- Make each eye movement slowly. Slow movement is the eye muscle strength training.

- Slowly look straight up, pause and then look straight down, pause. Repeat 3 - 5 times.

- Slowly look from side to side, pausing at the extremes 3 - 5 times. Hold your head still.

- Slowly look from the upper right corner to the lower left corner, pausing at the extremes. Repeat 3 -5 times.

- Slowly look from the upper left corner to the lower right corner, pausing at the extremes. Repeat 3 - 5 times.

- Keeping your eyes wide open, slowly circle your gaze all around, circling to the left, and then to the right. Repeat 3 times.

- Hold an index finger straight up out in front of you, with your elbow bent comfortably.

Practice gazing at the tip of your finger without blinking your eyes. Hold a steady gaze with both eyes focused on your finger tip. Try for a slow count of 50 before blinking.

This next exercise helps with focus elasticity. It is especially helpful when spending a lot of time at a computer, where the eyes get very little movement.

- Keep your head still, facing straight away. Only the eyes move.

- Look at the tip of your nose. Now look at a point in the distance.

- Switch your gaze from nose to distance and back again 10 – 20 times.

- Close your eyes and gently place the palms of your hands over them. Focus your gaze inward, with your thoughts on mute for a slow count from 1 to 30, or longer for greater stress relief.

THREE EASY FAVORITE SUBTLE-ENERGY EXERCISES

1. <u>BODY TAPPING</u>

<u>(Formally called "Emotional Freedom Technique" or EFT)</u>

- With palm of hand open, or with fingers folded over the palm (not a fist), gently tap in the center of your chest. This is the area of your Thymus Gland. The tapping sends a very healing vibration throughout your body. It always leaves one feeling better than before doing the tapping.

-With three fingers of each hand, tap along the lower edge of your collar bones. Tapping this area also sends a healing vibration throughout your body for relaxation.

-Next, with two fingers of each hand move along the lower edge of your collar bone, to the end points located at the base of your neck. Gently tap under the lower edge of these points for additional stress relief.

2. <u>FLUFFING ENERGY</u>

Hands out in front, palms facing your body, with elbows slightly bent. Open your palms with fingers spread apart. And if you can, pull your thumbs back a little, like bent wings, to further open your palms.

Now, with palms always facing your body, and in a relaxed motion, start making fluffing-like circles with your hands. The circle motion is an in and out motion in front of your body, as if you are fluffing the air between hands and body. Fluff from head to toe and back up again. Fluff around your head. Fluff again in the areas where it feels the best. This is a great energy booster. You may even give a deep sigh of release. Feel the feel of relief that follows. There may even be a tingly feeling here and there.

Check the illustration on the next page for a visual reference.

FIGURE 4 FLUFFING ENERGY

3. <u>ENERGY LIFTING SELF-HUG</u>

Young children, and some adults, practice this position quite naturally, without any training.

Stretch arms out in front -palms facing down -cross wrists and turn hands so that palms are facing -interlock fingers –bend elbows, drawing hands toward your chest –turn interlocked hands toward your chest and continue the turning motion till arms and hands are hugging your chest. Hold for as long as you feel comfortable in this position.

FIGURE 5 SELF-HUG

FUN FOR EVERYONE BONUS ACTIVITY

<u>MAKING BIG SOAP BUBBLES</u>

<u>Method 1</u>: Use a hoola hoop in a wading pool with enough soap to make bubbles –they are huge. Try getting inside the bubble by sitting or standing in the pool, and having another person pull the hoola hoop up to make the bubble.

<u>Method 2</u>: Hook the ends of a two-foot piece of plastic chain to the ends of one stick. Stretch about an eight-inch distance and attach that link to the end of a second stick. This will make a triangle shape when separating the stick ends.

Dip the chain into soap bubble water while holding the stick ends together. Lift the chain out of the water and separate the stick ends. Then move your arms in a slow circle-like flowing motion, along with taking some steps, to create a beautiful bubble tube.

COMFORTING WORDS FOR
FEELING AT PEACE

Breathing in slowly and deeply,
and then a brief pause before slowly exhaling,
pausing just a little longer before the next inhale.
Take a few more of these soothing breaths.
May you relax your tense muscles
and feel at peace in your heart-center,
feeling appreciation and gratitude
for all that is good and going well in your life this day.
And then, may you send out feelings of
good-will from your heart-center
for healing all of life, as you also bring healing
into your own loving, beautiful inner being.
May you feel at peace throughout your whole body.
Throughout your sense of being may you feel at Peace.
May you feel your inner-light radiate out with
joy, as a source of healing into all of life.
And from these individual actions,
may there be peaceful community
in the harmony in Earth.
May the heart-centers of people all around the Earth
join in the unity of sending love and good-will
to life in every form.
And so it is.

ACKNOWLEDGEMENTS

In honor of Louise Hay for her illumined teachings, so lovingly inspiring and uplifting countless lives. And, for holding true to her inner-ding while bringing Hay House publishing ever-forward through the years. A warm thank you to the Hay House team, who are always kind and service oriented. I especially thank Reid Tracy for your grounded strength in reason, serving as the guiding light at Hay House. And at Balboa Press Publishing, I am grateful for the team who kindly guided my steps into the world of published writing. Your support on this project has made it possible to bring a life-time of accumulated thoughts, ideas, experiences, and knowingness into print, to share with anyone who is seeking a happier life.

Printed in the United States
By Bookmasters